THE PROMISE OF THE FATHER

by Dr. Steve Schell

LIFE LESSONS
PUBLISHING

Original cover photo:
Cassandra Hamilton

Cover art:
Sandy Allnock
sandy@sandyallnock.com

Location:
Banias Falls, Israel

by Dr. C. Stevens Schell

Second Printing

LIFE LESSONS
PUBLISHING

A Registered Trade Name of
Pastoral Resource Ministry
Federal Way, Washington

ISBN: 978-1-7348135-4-8

Printed in the United States of America

Now on the last day,
the great day of the feast,
Jesus stood and cried out saying,
"If anone is thirsty, let him
come to Me and drink.
He who believes in Me as the
Scripture said, 'From his innermost
being will flow rivers of living water.'"

John 7:37-38

"And behold, I am sending forth
the promise of My Father upon you;
but you are to stay in the city until you are
clothed with power from on high."

Luke 24:49

A Word from the Author

As He prepared His disciples for His departure, Jesus was full of joyful anticipation. He could see His future church through the eyes of faith. He knew that His followers would soon be baptized with the Holy Spirit, and that meant that the powerful ministry He had been doing could be carried into the future by growing multitudes of men and women. In effect, He would continue His ministry through them. That was the plan. But sadly, when we read church history, we discover that His plan went unfulfilled at times. The baptism with the Holy Spirit was forgotten, and the gifts of the Spirit were ignored. Yet that doesn't change the fact that there was a plan. Nor does the failure by some in the past to walk in that plan mean it's no longer available to us today. It is! And I believe the revival we long for awaits those who will return to that original plan. My prayer is that this book will help that happen.

The Promise of the Father is divided into three sections. The first eleven chapters are designed to help us understand the baptism with the Holy Spirit and to learn how to receive it. We'll recognize that this gift of a new intimacy with God is a central element in His great plan for the human race. We'll observe some of the promises Jesus saw in the Old Testament and listen to John the Baptist introduce Jesus as the Baptizer with the Holy Spirit. We'll watch this promised era of the Spirit arrive after Jesus ascends into heaven. And then we'll turn our attention to practical insights that can help us receive this same gift, including a discussion of some of the obstacles that frequently hinder people. And in the final three chapters of this section, we will reflect on the profound changes the Holy Spirit works inside us.

The second section, "The Spirit and the Gathered Church," takes the reader passage by passage through chapters 12, 13 and 14 of First Corinthians. And the significance of these three chapters is profound: Nowhere else in the Bible is there a detailed description of how an apostolic church service functioned. These chapters are unique and invaluable. They give us a glimpse of what happened when the churches Paul planted gathered for worship, and therefore, can become a model for us today. Even though much of this material was written to correct wrong behavior, we are nonetheless listening to the apostle Paul coach people who had been baptized with the Holy Spirit on how to minister in the Spirit properly. He is so vivid in his language that it becomes possible to picture those services in our minds and then to allow the realities he taught them to guide our own gatherings. After all, the baptism with the Holy Spirit is meant to release all of God's people to function in the gifts of the Spirit. So by listening to what Paul taught to the church in Corinth, we too can learn how to minister together in the Spirit.

The third and final section is only one chapter, yet its message is important: It's the other bookend to God's great plan for the human race. It reminds us that we began in a garden surrounded by the Spirit but will end up in an eternal city where the glory of God is so intense, we wouldn't be able to physically tolerate it now. And that perspective clarifies the way we think about our relationship with the Holy Spirit. We recognize that a life of dependency on His power is what God always intended to be "normal" for us. So the baptism with the Holy Spirit should never be viewed as optional or available only to a few. It's meant to be a foundational part of every believer's equipment as a disciple of Jesus Christ. It's the beginning of the restoration of what God has always wanted to give us. It's our foretaste of the powers of the age to come. It's the firstfruits of the glorious future that's waiting for us.

Acknowledgements

This book began as a series of sermons about the Baptism with the Holy Spirit. For years I had been keeping a growing list of topics on this subject and was building an outline for a book. And then during the final year and a half of my pastoral ministry, I felt the Lord lead me to try to develop those ideas further by preaching them. When I started out, I made the decision to not set a time limit on the series but to take the time I needed to properly address key biblical passages and important insights. And as I mentioned, that series lasted a year and a half, and this is the book that came from it. I tell you these things because that kind of slow, methodical work would not have been possible without a very special group of people: the congregation and staff of Northwest Church. Someone once said, "The preacher doesn't build the church, the church builds the preacher," and I think I understand what that person meant. Mary and I had the privilege to serve a congregation that loved to hear the Word of God preached. And their passion actually pressed me to go deep, to not give shallow treatment to profound truths. So when some groups may have grown weary listening to so many sermons on one theme, Northwest Church only encouraged me, from the staff who set up the services, managed the sound, and typed and printed the sermon notes, to the members who prayed for their preacher and gave so generously to see that this book could be published. To all of you I say thank you! This could not have happened without you.

Nor could it have happened without my amazing family. This kind of writing takes a lot of time and has often left me weary or caused me to show up late to special gatherings. Yet you unwaveringly loved me and believed in what I was doing. Your faith and your patience have always been a foundation for me and still are. There simply aren't words to express how grateful I am for all of you!

Nobody writes a book alone. It takes many people contributing at many levels to produce something that can actually help others. And I'm especially conscious of that fact when it comes to this book. In fact, I hardly know where to start, but here goes: Lianna Greer, you didn't just type my illegible handwritten sermons; you put your heart into it and did it with great care and precision. I have no idea how many of the sermon titles you helped me choose. Thank you! Martina Cline, you carefully kept track of all the various documents because you care so deeply about the people they will help. Thank you! Leigh Harris, it's a joy to work with someone who is so passionate about the effectiveness of this book. Your tireless proofreading and heartfelt feedback changed the book in many ways and made it much better. Thank you! Katrin Hagman, your literary insight helped to pull an assortment of sermons into a readable book. You shepherded this project beautifully. You're a gifted teacher, administrator and grammarian all in one. Thank you! Fred Renich at Pine Hill Graphics, your skill and encouragement in guiding the whole publishing process is a gift to us. Thank you! Keri Welch, your gift as a graphic designer made this book beautiful. Thank you! Sandy Allnock, how beautifully you captured the overflowing joy of having the Holy Spirit dwell in us in the painting that became our front cover. Your art is a powerful voice! Thank you for sharing it with us. Cassandra Hamilton, your beautiful photograph of Banias Falls in Israel was the inspiration for Sandy's art work. Thank you! Rick Battershell, it was your seasoned wisdom and generous heart that guided the formation of Pastoral Resource Ministry and Life Lessons Publishing. Thank you! And finally, Mary Schell, for serving as our financial officer, wise advisor, steadfast prayer warrior, and daily encourager, I thank you from the bottom of my heart!

Book Abbreviations

Ge - Genesis
Ex - Exodus
Lev - Leviticus
Nu - Numbers
Dt - Deuteronomy
Jos - Joshua
Jdg - Judges
Ru - Ruth
1Sa - 1 Samuel
2Sa - 2 Samuel
1Ki - 1 Kings
2Ki - 2 Kings
1Ch - 1 Chronicles
2Ch - 2 Chronicles
Ezr - Ezra
Ne - Nehemiah
Est - Esther
Job - Job
Ps - Psalms
Pr - Proverbs
Ecc - Ecclesiastes
SS - Song of Solomon
Isa - Isaiah
Jer - Jeremiah
La - Lamentations
Eze - Ezekiel
Da - Daniel
Hos - Hosea
Joel - Joel
Am - Amos
Ob - Obadiah
Jnh - Jonah
Mic - Micah
Na - Nahum
Hab - Habakkuk
Zep - Zephaniah
Hag - Haggai
Zec - Zechariah
Mal - Malachi
Mt - Matthew
Mk - Mark
Lk - Luke
Jn - John
Ac - Acts
Ro - Romans
1Co - 1 Corinthians
2Co - 2 Corinthians
Gal - Galatians
Eph - Ephesians
Php - Philippians
Col - Colossians
1Th - 1 Thessalonians
2Th - 2 Thessalonians
1Ti - 1 Timothy
2Ti - 2 Timothy
Titus - Titus
Phm - Philemon
Heb - Hebrews
Jas - James
1Pe - 1 Peter
2Pe - 2 Peter
1Jn - 1 John
2Jn - 2 John
3Jn - 3 John
Jude - Jude
Rev - Revelation

Table of Contents

Section Three

The Order of Future Events

A Personal Note

Before you read any further, there is something you should know. I was baptized with the Holy Spirit when I was 12 years old, and the impact of that encounter is still with me over six decades later. It changed me so deeply that I'm still trying to understand what happened that day. I tell you this now so you'll know before you start that when it comes to the subject of the baptism with the Holy Spirit, I am fully persuaded that it is real, wonderful and available to all who believe in the Lord Jesus Christ. And I openly admit that the goal of this book is to convince you of this, if you were uncertain, and help you receive it if you wish to. Yet having said that, I want to assure you that I am committed to being completely honest with the Bible. I've earnestly tried to view each passage in its proper context and not distort its intended meaning. So if you've had some longstanding questions about this subject, I think you may find some fresh answers here, and if you've been hungry for what Jesus calls "the promise of My Father," please keep reading because that promise is real, wonderful and waiting for you.

Section One

The Baptism with the Holy Spirit

The chapters in this section are meant to lay a foundation of understanding about the baptism with the Holy Spirit. They cover a wide range of topics, but each topic has been carefully selected in order to answer a significant question about this subject. Taken together they provide a broad, biblical perspective. The reader will find here answers to such questions as: Who is the Holy Spirit; Why do humans desperately need Him; Which Old Testament promise did Jesus refer to as "the promise of My Father"; How important is the baptism with the Holy Spirit to God's purpose in sending Jesus; What actually happened to the disciples on the Day of Pentecost; How do we receive this gift today; Why does speaking in tongues matter; Did Paul say these tongues would cease when the Bible was finished being written; Where do we find the power to live the new life Jesus offers us; and finally, How does the Holy Spirit prove to us and others that we belong to God?

Gathering them together, He commanded them
not to leave Jerusalem, but to wait
for what the Father had promised,
"Which," He said, "you heard of from me;
for John baptized with water,
but you will be baptized with the Holy Spirit
not many days from now."

Acts 1:4-5

Chapter One

The Holy Spirit

The human race was never designed to function without the Holy Spirit! The first humans were surrounded by His presence, and at the end of time redeemed humanity will live in a city lighted by the glory of God. In this first lesson we will try to answer the foundational question: Who is the Holy Spirit? And then we'll reflect on how our relationship with Him was lost, and how Jesus' death and resurrection began the process of restoring that relationship.

Who is the Holy Spirit?

That question is more difficult to answer than one would expect because when we try to understand this person of God, we encounter an element of mystery. We meet Him in the second verse of the Bible. The first tells us that God created the heavens and the earth, but the next verse explains that it was the "Spirit of God" who hovered over the surface of the waters in a world that was formless and empty (Ge 1:2). And then as we continue to read on through the Bible, we encounter many references to Him, yet in the Old Testament we find no clear definition of who He is. We are left to wonder whether or not the authors are speaking about a separate person of God or merely using the term "Spirit of God" as another way of saying "God." It seems uncertain as to whether the title "Spirit of God" is simply referring to the active presence of God the Father at work in a particular situation or whether it is pointing to a distinct person, separate from though equal in nature to the Father. Here are a few examples of such passages:

During the Exodus the Lord caused a man named Bezalel to be filled "with the Spirit of God, in wisdom, in understanding and in knowledge and in all craftsmanship" (Ex 35:31).

On another occasion the Lord "took of the Spirit who was upon him [Moses] and placed [Him] upon seventy elders. And when the Spirit rested upon them, they prophesied" (Nu 11:25).

Later, the Spirit of the Lord came upon Israel's judges, and when He did, they became bold and strong (Jdg 11:29; 14:6).

When the Spirit of the Lord came upon Saul, he prophesied (1Sa 10:6, 10).

The Spirit of the Lord came mightily upon David when the prophet Samuel anointed him with oil (1Sa 16:13).

After sinning with Bathsheba David begged God not to take His Holy Spirit from him (Ps 51:11).

Isaiah prophesied that the "Spirit of the Lord" would rest upon the Messiah, and His presence would bring to Him wisdom, understanding, counsel, strength, knowledge and the fear of the Lord (Isa 11:2).

Isaiah also prophesied that when the kingdom of God arrived, the Spirit would be poured out upon the earth, and the wilderness would become a fertile field (Isa 32:15).

He said the whole earth would be immersed in the presence of God's Spirit like the waters cover the sea (Isa 11:9). And Habakkuk said the same thing (Hab 2:14).

Through Isaiah we hear the Messiah declare that He can proclaim God's message because the "Spirit of the Lord" is upon Him (Isa 61:1; Lk 4:17-18).

Ezekiel prophesied that a day would come when God would place His Spirit inside His people (Eze 36:27; 37:14).

> And Joel prophesied that in the last days God would pour out His Spirit on all humans, whether male or female, whether young or old (Joel 2:28).

In these passages the Holy Spirit is always spoken of as the Lord's Spirit or the Spirit of God. God sends Him upon people, and it is by His power that God ministers through people. So there is no question that the Old Testament recognizes that there is a Spirit of God, but that He is a distinct person and not an emanation of the Father is not easily discernable.

However, that uncertainty disappears when we arrive at the New Testament. Here the Holy Spirit is spoken of often with many passages speaking of Him in a way that indicates that He is a distinct person of God. Here are some examples:

> Joseph was told by an angel that the child in Mary had been conceived by the Holy Spirit (Mt 1:20).

> John the Baptist prophesied that the coming Messiah would baptize people with the Holy Spirit like he baptized people with water (Mt 3:11).

> Then he saw the Spirit of God descend from heaven and alight on Jesus like a dove, and heard the Father say, "This is My beloved Son, in whom I am well-pleased" (Mt 3:16-17).

> The resurrected Jesus told His followers to make disciples by "baptizing them in the name of the Father and the Son and the Holy Spirit" (Mt 28:19).

> And on the day of Pentecost believers were filled with the Holy Spirit and began to speak in tongues (Ac 2:4).

But it is when we come to the gospel of John that the person and role of the Holy Spirit are seen most clearly. Through John we hear Jesus announce that after He has been raised from the dead, His disciples would have God's presence dwelling within them by means of the Holy Spirit (Jn 4:14; 7:37-39; 14:16-20, 23). And it's in John's gospel that we hear Him describe the

Holy Spirit as a person distinct from the Father and Himself. In John 14:16 He makes that distinction indisputably clear. He refers to the Holy Spirit as "another Helper" (Greek: allon parakleton) using the Greek word which means "another of the same kind" (allos) rather than the word which means "another of a different kind" (heteros). And He repeatedly uses the masculine, demonstrative pronoun ("that one") when referring to the Holy Spirit (Jn 14:26; 15:26; 16:13-14). He promises His followers that He will ask the Father for the Spirit so that He can send Him to them (Jn 14:16). And then after being resurrected He breathed on His disciples and said, "Receive the Holy Spirit," symbolizing that the Holy Spirit would be given to them through Him (Jn 20:22), and that the gift began to arrive on the day of Pentecost (Ac 2:1-4).

And here is an important point to remember: Since Jesus is the only-begotten God (Jn 1:14, 18), the divine Son, who came from heaven to become a man (Jn 3:13, 16), when He reveals a spiritual truth, those of us who believe in Him must consider that truth to be a settled matter. So whether or not we fully understand all that He has revealed to us about the Holy Spirit, we still choose to believe everything He said. And He said the Holy Spirit is another person of God, distinct from the Father and Himself. So though there are many passages in the Bible that teach us about the Holy Spirit, it is Jesus Himself who finally removes all doubt that there are three persons within the presence and power whom we call God: There is a Father from whom all things have come and for whom all things exist; there is a Son who was begotten by the Father and so fully shares His divine nature; and there is a Holy Spirit who is also fully divine but whose origin remains a mystery. In John 15:26 Jesus gives us one of the most revealing statements found in Scripture. He says the Holy Spirit, whom He calls "the Spirit of Truth," proceeds from the Father. The Greek literally reads: "He goes out from beside the Father." We learn from this verse that the Holy Spirit has been sent to us from the Father, through the Son, and that His presence within us enables us to represent and declare Jesus accurately and powerfully (Jn 15:26-27; 16:13-15).

Once we recognize that Jesus has revealed that our God is a community of three persons who are all of the same, divine nature and capacity, then we must recognize that each of those persons has a different role. The Father is the Source of all things and the One for whom all things exist, which is why the goal of the entire Bible is to restore our relationship with Him. The

Son is the One through whom the Father spoke creation into existence (Jn 1:2-3, 10) and to whom, because of His willing sacrifice of Himself on the cross, the Father now commands all creation to submit (Php 2:9-11). And as the resurrected Lord He is now in the process of bringing all creation into submission to Himself so that when His work is finished, He can present a restored creation back to the Father so that the Father will receive the supreme honor that belongs to Him (1Co 15:24-28). The Holy Spirit is the One by whom many of the works of God are performed, whether it be the creation of the material world, the forming of godly character in a believer's life, the provision of supernatural gifts to enable the believer to minister effectively, or the glorious transformation of this planet in the age to come. He is the "Hand" of God by whom these works are accomplished. And it is His presence within us that continually assists our human spirit to pray accurately (Jn 14:20, 23; Ro 8:26-27). He is the One who actively comforts, guides, convicts and counsels us, but He does so in such a way that our experience of God is seamless. Because there is perfect unity between the Father, Son and Holy Spirit, there is no difference between them in will, capacity or character. Among them there is only one will, and that is the will of the Father. The Son constantly points us to the Father, and the Holy Spirit constantly helps us understand and obey the Son. So we experience God as one, consistent person. And as we've seen, Scripture shows that within this One, whom we call God, there is a community of three persons: Father, Son and Holy Spirit who are one in nature and one in purpose.

Restoring what was lost

You and I were designed by God to live in the presence of the Holy Spirit like fish immersed in water. He placed the first man and woman in a garden full of His presence, and the beautiful light of that presence may have served to "clothe" them because they didn't discover they were naked until after they sinned (Ge 3:7). By making them in His own image and likeness, God made them intelligent, rational and (initially) pure beings. He gave them the capacity to make choices, whether right or wrong, as well as genuine emotions so they could feel joy, sorrow and, above all, love. But with that gift of freedom came the danger that they would not obey Him. Yet because His goal for them was that they would become truly good, not just innocent, they had to be given the opportunity to make moral choices. It's very important to note that God did not create humans without a will or place them in an environment where they had no opportunity to disobey. He strategically placed the tree of the knowledge of good and evil in the center of the garden and then told them not to eat from it so that their will would be tested (Ge 2:17).

But sadly they chose to eat its fruit, and one of the terrible changes that occurred after that act of rebellion was that the presence of the Holy Spirit departed from them. That light that may have clothed them was gone, and for the first time in their lives they were spiritually alone. Though God was present in the garden, to them He became distant. Their sin had made them unclean, and their bodies had become an unsuitable place for a Holy Spirit to dwell. From now on their natural tendency would always be to function in their own strength and make decisions based on their own wisdom. They could still turn to God for help, but it was now much more difficult to hear His voice and obey. And that kind of dependence and obedience would become rare among their descendants. The unhindered intimacy they originally had with God was gone. The ease of communication that had allowed them to openly converse with Him was gone. No longer did His intense presence infuse life into every cell of their beings and empower them to think clearly. So they began to make more wrong choices, and their bodies began to die.

Initially it appeared that God's plan for the human race had been spoiled. He had created them with the goal that they would become His adopted children: that they would love Him, obey Him, glorify Him and enjoy Him forever. But by misusing their God-given freedom, they had separated themselves from the Source that would make that plan possible, and unless that relationship could be restored, the plan would be lost forever. Yet God always returns to His original goal. He doesn't change His goals. He reaches them by another way. That's true because the original was perfect, and His great goodness cannot allow Him to compromise something that is pure and complete and replace it with something that is not. To do so would contaminate something that is holy, which is why the Bible is a progressive history of redemption.

Once the original plan for the human race was damaged, God immediately began to guide us back to Himself, back to His original plan and back to the intimacy which He originally intended for us. And He won't be defeated. What was lost must be restored, which means humans must once again be clothed with the power of God (Lk 24:49). The Old Testament repeatedly teaches that the glorious presence of the Holy Spirit will be given back to God's people in the age to come, and the New Testament reveals that the cross and resurrection of Jesus Christ have made it possible for the Holy Spirit to return to us now. The restoration of what was lost has already begun. You might say that Jesus has made it possible for the powers of the age to come to break into the darkness of this present age (Heb 6:4-5). And though you and I still live in a dying world, the glory that will be fully given to us in the future has already begun to arrive. The original plan is being restored. Jesus' cross and resurrection did not just forgive our sins; He gave us back "the right to become children of God" (Jn 1:12).

Conclusion

Once we understand God's great plan, the importance of receiving the Holy Spirit's presence into our lives becomes obvious. Learning to listen to the voice of God and depend on Him as our Source was never meant to be optional; it was always meant to be foundational. So it is wonderful when we read the Word of God and discover that the Holy Spirit has again been made available to us. What was lost has been rescued. The relationship that we had in the garden of Eden has been made possible again, and at an even more profound level. Because of the cross and resurrection, the Father and Son can abide with us (Jn 14:23) and send the Holy Spirit to dwell within us (Jn14:17; 15:26). Because of Jesus we can experience the "glory" God wanted to give us when He made us.

Chapter Two

The Promise of the Spirit

Jesus clearly believed that His disciples would be given a new relationship with the Holy Spirit after His death and resurrection, and He based that belief on promises He saw in the Old Testament. There was an excitement and even joy in the way He assured them that something new was coming that would elevate them to a far greater ministry potential than the world had ever seen. In the future they would be able to minister as powerfully as He did. He called this, "The Promise of the Father" (Lk 24:49; Ac 1:4).

Preparing for His presence

A holy God cannot dwell in an unholy place. Everything about Him is pure, loving, just and good. So if humans want Him to come and live among us with all of our impurity, lovelessness, injustice and evil, we must prepare a place that's suitable for Him. And if we understand that principle, we will understand why God gave Moses such careful instructions about the tabernacle in the wilderness. In order for God to accompany His people as they traveled toward the Promised Land, they needed to prepare a place for Him that was not contaminated by influences or objects that He found offensive. He told Moses, "Let them construct a sanctuary for Me, that I may dwell among them" (Ex 25:8). If the people of Israel would obey His commandments, He promised to bless them in many ways, but none greater than this: "I will make My dwelling among you, and My soul will not reject you. I will also walk among you and be your God, and you shall be My people" (Lev 26:11-12). Later on, when Solomon built the temple, God said to him, "[Concerning] this house which you are building, if you will walk in My statutes and execute My ordinances and keep all My commandments by walking in them, then I will carry out My Word with you which I spoke to David your father. I will dwell among the sons of Israel, and I will not forsake My people Israel" (1Ki 6:12-13).

Yet it would not be enough for Israel to merely build a physical space where God could dwell. He also required them to prepare themselves. When He met with the nation at Mount Sinai, He made a covenant with them which contained hundreds of commandments designed to elevate their behavior and attitudes until they became holy like He was holy. The rules He gave them taught them how to worship Him and how to relate to one another. He said the goal of those rules was to cause them to be devoted to Him and to become like Him: "Thus you are to be holy to Me, for I the Lord am holy; and I have set you apart from the peoples to be Mine" (Lev 20:26).

If God's people would prepare a place for Him to dwell, and if they themselves would become holy, He would come to live among them, and with His presence would come "shalom" (peace), which is the infusion of life that takes place in everything and everybody when God Himself is near.

A lack of power

However, it didn't take long for Israel to discover that the Law that God gave to Moses at Mount Sinai was not able to make them truly holy. It could teach them what was right, but it could not empower them to do what was right. It could not stop the wrong desires that arise in the human heart or empower a person to resist those desires when they arose. It could command someone to love their neighbor, but it could not supply the love they would need to actually do it. It could command someone not to lust, but not bring relief from the temptation. It could command a person not to kill, but not stop those surges of anger that swell up inside a person and produce murderous thoughts. No matter how successfully someone obeyed its rules about external behavior, it gave them no power to bring internal attitudes or emotions into obedience. Even in the most zealous law-keeper outward obedience is always spoiled by inward disobedience. All who are honest with themselves are forced to admit that they are unable to love as they ought to love or remain pure in the face of temptation or forgive offenses completely. And all of this failure naturally creates a great deal of frustration. Those who are bold enough to look within and honestly evaluate what they see there have to face the fact that they possess attitudes that fall short of God's standard and deserve judgment. But those who hide wrong attitudes and pretend they don't exist become hypocrites. In either case the Law condemns us all as sinners.

The Sermon on the Mount

This distinction between these inner and outer aspects of a person's obedience to God is addressed by Jesus in the Sermon on the Mount. He points to certain commands in the Law of Moses that people inevitably fail to obey inwardly even if they are able to obey them outwardly. Here is an example:

> "You have heard that the ancients were told, 'You shall not commit murder' and 'Whoever commits murder shall be liable to the court.' But I say to you that everyone who is angry with his brother shall be guilty before the court; and whoever says to his brother, 'You good-for-nothing,' shall be guilty before the supreme court; and whoever says, 'You fool,' shall be guilty [enough to go] into the fiery hell" (Mt 5:21- 22).

And He warns His listeners that God expects them to obey His laws internally as well as externally. It wasn't enough that they had not intentionally killed someone. If they had grown angry (Greek: orge) to the point of wishing for revenge (W.E. Vine, Expository Dictionary of New Testament Words, Volume 1, "orge," pp. 55-56, Fleming H. Revell Company, p1966) or had said something degrading about another person, Jesus' sermon forced them to admit that by God's standards they were murderers. His purpose in doing this was to show those who were trying to become righteous by keeping God's Law that they could not succeed. Even those who obeyed it externally inevitably failed internally. And He was not trying to shame His listeners; He was trying to awaken them to their desperate need for God's mercy. His words were meant to destroy any hope to which they might be clinging that when they stood before God at the final judgment, He would reckon them to be sinless. Jesus was deliberately driving them and us into the arms of grace.

Paul's testimony

Paul briefly summarizes his own journey toward this realization that he was unable to meet the standards of God's Law in his letter to the church in Rome. In chapter seven he describes how the Law forced him to admit that he was a sinner. He says up to a certain point in his life he believed he was successfully keeping the Law (Ro 7:9; Php 3:6), but then a moment came when he tried to obey a particular, internal command, the one that says, "You shall not covet" (lust), and he discovered that he was unable to restrain it. In fact the harder he tried not to covet the more that evil desire grew (Ro 7:7-8). Then after using himself as an example of human inability to obey God's Law, he explains that God knew humans would be unable to obey His Law even before He sent it, but He sent it anyway so we would discover how much we needed His forgiveness <u>and</u> the power of the Holy Spirit.

The Father's promise

How is it possible that after sending His Law to show us our sin and expose how unfit we are to dwell in His presence God would announce through His prophets that a day would come when He would dwell <u>inside</u> His people? If a holy God cannot dwell in an unholy place, and the human race has proven that not one of us is able to meet the standards of His Law, then how could that ever happen? And yet He said it would. Listen to Jeremiah, Ezekiel and Joel:

> "Behold, days are coming," declares the Lord, "when I will make a <u>new covenant</u> with the house of Israel and with the house of Judah, not like the covenant which I made with their fathers in the day I took them by the hand to bring them out of the land of Egypt, My covenant which they broke, although I was a husband to them," declares the Lord. "But this is the covenant which I will make with the house of Israel after those days," [see Dt 30:1-6] declares the Lord, "I will put My law within them and on their heart I will write it; and I will be their God, and they shall be My people. They shall not teach again, each man his neighbor, and each man his brother, saying, 'Know the Lord,' for they will all know Me, from the least of them to the greatest of them," declares the Lord, "for I will forgive their

> iniquity, and their sin I will remember no more" (Jer 31:31-34; see Heb 8:8-12).

> "For I will take you [Israel] from the nations, gather you from all the lands and bring you into your own land. Then I will sprinkle clean water on you, and you will be clean; I will cleanse you from all your filthiness and from all your idols. Moreover, I will give you a new heart and put a new spirit within you; and I will remove the heart of stone from your flesh and give you a heart of flesh. I will put My Spirit <u>within</u> [Hebrew: gereb, inside the body] you and cause you to walk in My statues, and you will be careful to observe My ordinances" (Eze 36:24-27).

> "It will come about after this [Israel's repentance and restoration at the coming of Messiah] That I will pour out My Spirit on all mankind [flesh]; And your sons and daughters will prophesy, Your old men will dream dreams, Your young men will see visions. Even on the male and female servants I will pour out My Spirit in those days" (Joel 2:28-29).

The Son's promise

Repeatedly during His ministry on earth Jesus promised that this new covenant with its outpouring and indwelling of the Holy Spirit would be given to His followers <u>after</u> He was crucified, resurrected and had ascended into heaven. He told His disciples that what He was about to do would bring the "promise of the Father," meaning that His cross would remove our uncleanness so that God Himself could come to dwell, not only <u>with</u> us, but literally <u>inside</u> us. In effect, Jesus said He would prepare us to be a holy place, a suitable habitation, a clean "tabernacle" where God could dwell. Listen to how He said this:

> "...Jesus stood and cried out, saying, 'If anyone is thirsty, let Him come to Me and drink. He who believes in Me, as the Scriptures said, "From his innermost being [Greek: koilia, inside the body cavity] will flow rivers of living water."' But this He spoke of the Spirit whom those who believed in Him were

> to receive; for the Spirit was not yet [given], because Jesus was not yet glorified" (Jn 7:37-39).
>
> "I will ask the Father, and He will give you another Helper, that He may be with you forever; [that is] the Spirit of truth whom the world cannot receive, because it does not see Him or know Him, [but] you know Him because He abides with you and will be in you" (Jn 14:16-17).
>
> "And behold, I am sending forth the promise of My Father upon you; but you are to stay in the city until you are clothed with power from on high" (Lk 24:49).

On the day He ascended into heaven, the resurrected Jesus commanded His disciples to wait in Jerusalem for what He called "the promise of the Father" (Ac 1:4). And He reminded them that He had already spoken to them about that promise many times during the years He ministered with them. The quotations listed above are examples of what He would say. And then, so no one would mistake which promise He meant when He used the term "the promise of the Father," He pictured what was going to happen to His disciples when it arrived. He said what God would do was similar to what John the Baptist had done when he immersed people in water, but instead of water, God would immerse them in the Holy Spirit, and He said this new relationship with the Holy Spirit had been prophesied by the prophets of Israel. And when we read the second chapter of Acts, we observe that "baptism" arrive ten days later on the day of Pentecost (Ac 2:1-4) and hear Peter announce that from that moment on it will be offered to all who call on the name of the Lord Jesus (Ac 2:37-39).

Receiving the promise

But how is this possible? How can a holy God dwell inside people whom the Law condemns, people who are unclean in their thoughts even when they manage to bring their outward behavior into obedience to the Law? Jesus revealed the answer to that question on the evening He was betrayed. He and His disciples ate a Passover meal together, and when the meal was finished, He picked up a special cup, one that was meant to be taken at that point in the ceremony, and filled it with wine. Then He said, "This cup which is poured out for you is the new covenant in My blood" (Lk 22:20), and He passed that cup to them. By doing so He was asking them to believe that because of the death He was about to die on the cross (His blood), they would receive the "new covenant" promised by the prophets. By using the term "new covenant" He was especially pointing them to the words of Jeremiah 31:31-34, quoted above. If a disciple drank the cup, it meant he believed his sins would be forgiven and remembered no more, that God would take out his heart of stone and give him a new heart that loved God and longed to obey Him, and that the Holy Spirit would come to dwell inside him and teach him to walk in God's ways. By drinking the cup he was saying to Jesus, "I believe this!" And when you and I drink this cup today, we say the same thing.

In his letter to the church in Rome Paul explains what Jesus did to make this new covenant possible. He tells us why the Holy Spirit is now able to dwell inside unholy bodies. Listen: "For what the Law could not do, weak as it was through the flesh, God [did]; sending His own Son in the likeness of sinful flesh and [as an offering] for sin, He condemned sin in the flesh, so that the requirement of the Law [which is perfect holiness in actions and attitudes] might be fulfilled in us, who do not walk according to the flesh but according to the Spirit" (Ro 8:3-4). In other words, by becoming a man and dying on the cross Jesus spiritually cleansed the flesh of our bodies which allows the Spirit to live inside us. Though the flesh of our bodies is still rebellious and dying, by faith we are joined to Jesus and share in His holiness, and because we share in His holiness, the Holy Spirit does not depart from us even when we sin. He remains inside us and provides the power we need to obey God. So maturing in the Christian life involves learning to stop listening to the voice of the flesh and start listening to the voice of the Spirit.

The good news

Here's the good news: When you and I place our faith in Jesus Christ, we are joined to Him spiritually. That means in God's eyes we died with Christ when He died on the cross and rose with Him when He was resurrected from the grave. So not only has the price for our sins been paid so that our human spirit is no longer separated from God, but the very flesh of our body has also been cleansed so that our physical body has become a suitable habitation for the Holy Spirit. For those who are joined to Christ, there is no longer any spiritual barrier between them and God, and their body is a clean temple in which His presence can dwell. You and I need to lay hold of those truths and not let go because all of us are painfully aware that we fail at times to obey God's holy standards, both externally by our actions and internally by our wrong attitudes and emotions.

If we lose sight of what Jesus' death and resurrection provide us, we can fall back under condemnation and assume that His presence has left us. So especially in those sorts of moments we must remind ourselves that we are clean because of Jesus' death on the cross, not because we successfully kept the Law. And it is only because of Jesus that the Holy Spirit is able to dwell in our "innermost being." We must not allow a troubled conscience to prevent us from welcoming God's power to strengthen us in our weakest moments. We must choose to believe what the prophets promised. We must choose to believe what Jesus announced. We must study until we understand what Paul explained to the Roman church. And if we do this, then we will trust in the continuous atonement of Jesus Christ so that when we sin, we won't think that the Spirit has left us. We will know He is there to restore us. We will know that even when we fail, we are clean before God because we are joined to the One who is clean, the Holy One of God, our Lord Jesus. If we understand that fact, it will encourage us to confess our sins quickly and boldly call on the Spirit to come and help us.

A pillar of fire (Ac 2:3)

On the day of Pentecost a pillar of fire appeared over each disciple's head, and that pillar of fire was a symbol every Jewish believer would have recognized immediately. They had been taught since they were children that when Moses prepared the tabernacle in the wilderness, the Lord demonstrated that He had come to dwell in that tabernacle by placing over it a cloud by day and a pillar of fire by night (Ex 40:34-38). So on Pentecost when fire appeared over every head, those disciples understood what God was saying to them: "This is now My tabernacle. It has been prepared for My presence and is clean. Here is My dwelling place." Do you and I believe that there is a pillar of fire over our head?

Chapter Three

Introducing Jesus

John 1:19-37

How important is the baptism with the Holy Spirit to God's purpose in sending His Son to earth? The man God prepared to introduce Jesus to the world made it one of the main truths he proclaimed about Him. John the Baptist called Jesus, "...the Lamb of God who takes away the sin of the world" (Jn 1:29), and then he said, "...this is the One who baptizes in the Holy Spirit" (Jn 1:33). If John saw the importance of Jesus as the Baptizer with the Holy Spirit, shouldn't we?

There are those who try to solve the puzzle of doctrinal differences about who Jesus is by saying, "Can't we all agree to simply believe in Jesus and ignore the issues that divide us?" And of course, we can as long as we're all talking about the same Jesus. But different people can believe very different things about Him. What one person might mean when they say His name may be very unlike what someone else means when they say that same name. In effect they may be speaking about two completely different people. If indeed we all meant the same thing when we spoke of Jesus, if we were all able to agree on the essential truths about Him, then we could set aside other differences and rest in the fact that we still share a common faith. And thankfully, there are many different groups within the family of God who do agree on these essential truths, but the religious world at large is not that simple. Countless teachers and traditions define Jesus in ways that are not in alignment with what the Bible teaches. They reinterpret Him to fit their own desires. It's actually overwhelming to stop and reflect on the enormous number of voices today proclaiming vastly different things about our Savior. And sadly this confusion is so prevalent that a sincere seeker of truth can easily become misled if they enter the religious arena without help to discern between what's true and what's false.

But thankfully there is a way to discover the truth about Jesus. It begins when a person accepts the Bible as the Word of God and then chooses to study it with humility and courage. Because when someone listens to the Bible like that, he or she will find in its pages the real Jesus. Any earnest seeker of truth will hear there the voices of those God selected to teach us about His Son, and one of the most important voices was that of a man named John the Baptist. So let's meet that man and listen to what he said when he introduced Jesus to the world, because in that introduction he presented four essential truths that everyone must believe in order to believe in the real Jesus.

John the Baptist

Who was John the Baptist, and why is he such an important voice in telling us about Jesus? The apostle John was this man's disciple before he became Jesus' disciple, and here's what the apostle John said about John the Baptist: "There came a man sent from God, whose name was John. He came as a witness, to testify about the Light, so that all might believe through him. He was not the Light, but [he came] to testify about the Light" (Jn 1:6-8). In other words, God sent John the Baptist to Israel and into the pages of the Bible with a very special assignment: Like a witness in a courtroom he was to stand before the whole world and declare the truth about Jesus. The apostle John is telling us that God uniquely prepared this special person to introduce His Son to those who want to know the truth about Him. That means that of all the voices in the world, other than the voice of Jesus Himself, to whom we ought to listen when that person tells us who Jesus is, that trustworthy voice is John the Baptist.

To begin with, the fact that John the Baptist ever existed was a miracle. Apart from the supernatural power of God he would never have been born. He was the child of a very old couple who were not able to conceive until an angel appeared to his father while he was performing priestly service in the temple. The angel told his father that he and his wife would have a son and that their son would prepare people to receive the Messiah. He also said their son would minister in the spirit and power of Elijah (Lk 1:11-17). And when their son was born, John's father prophesied these words: "And you, child, will be called the prophet of the Most High; for you will go on before the Lord to prepare His ways; to give to His people [the] knowledge of salvation by the forgiveness of their sins…" (Lk 1:76-77). And Luke gives us more information about John's upbringing. He says, "…the child continued to grow and to become strong in spirit, and he lived in the deserts until the day of his public appearance to Israel" (Lk 1:80).

John's unique role as the prophet sent by God to introduce Jesus is also confirmed by the fact that not only did John testify about Jesus, but Jesus testified about John. And here's what Jesus said about him: "This is the one about whom it is written, 'Behold, I send My messenger ahead of You, who will prepare Your way before You'. Truly I say to you, among those born of women there has not arisen [anyone] greater than John the Baptist!... For all the prophets and the Law prophesied until John. And if you are willing to accept [it], John himself is Elijah who was to come" (Mt 11:10-14 quoting Mal 3:1). Jesus was unmistakably announcing that John was the "forerunner" about whom the prophet Malachi had written. He was the messenger whom God had promised to send in the boldness and power of Elijah to prepare the hearts of Israel to receive their true Messiah. And the success of John's ministry can be seen by the fact that when Jesus began to minister publicly, the multitudes who had been following John left him and began to follow Jesus. When that happened, instead of feeling jealous John rejoiced (Jn 3:26-30). He understood this was what was supposed to happen, and that response reveals a remarkable level of humility and the clarity of his faith. Not only was he not surprised that the Messiah had come, he had been fully expecting Him to arrive in his lifetime. In fact, John had been preaching about the Messiah so powerfully that many of his listeners had begun to wonder if he were the Messiah, rather than the Messiah's forerunner. But he fervently denied it saying he was only "…a voice of one crying in the wilderness, 'Make straight the way of the Lord,' as Isaiah the prophet said" (Jn 1:23 quoting Isa 40:3).

Introducing Jesus

So what did John the Baptist say about Jesus? How did this special vessel prepared by God, this "voice crying in the wilderness," introduce Him? I believe that special moment, when he made his great introduction, took place about forty days after Jesus was baptized in the Jordan River. He may have looked up at the very moment Jesus was returning from His temptation in the nearby Judean wilderness. The apostle John, who was present when this encounter happened, tells us that the great prophet saw Jesus coming toward him, and the first thing he said was, "Behold, the Lamb of God who takes away the sin of the world" (Jn 1:29). To John the Baptist, and all those who heard him that day, his use of the word "lamb," particularly a lamb that "takes away the sin of the world," was an unmistakable reference to the lambs used in Israel's ritual sacrifices in the temple. In other words John pointed at Jesus and announced to everyone that the moral guilt of the entire human race was going to be transferred onto Jesus. Like the lamb eaten at the Passover meal (Ex 12:3-11), or one of the lambs sacrificed on the altar of burnt offering, Jesus had been sent by God to die as the substitute for the world's sin and to rescue all who believe in Him from eternal judgment.

Then after making this first stunning announcement, John immediately made a second announcement that was equally as stunning. He said, "This is He concerning whom I said, 'The One who comes after me is greater than me for He existed before me'" (Jn 1:15, literal). Basically, he pointed at Jesus and said, "This man pre-existed His human birth." And that's clearly what the apostle John understood him to say because he quotes these words in the introduction to his gospel. There he explains that Jesus is God's divine Son who existed in heaven <u>before</u> He became a man, and one of the proofs he uses to support this claim is the statement made by John the Baptist that day.

After calling Jesus the "Lamb of God" and telling everyone Jesus pre-existed His human birth, John announced a third essential truth. He said that God had informed him earlier in his ministry that he was to watch carefully because the Messiah would come to him to be baptized, and when He did, God would show John that this was indeed the Messiah by a very specific sign. John would see the Holy Spirit descend from heaven and remain on Him (see Jn 1:33). And when John introduced Jesus that day, he explained to the crowd that he saw that happen when he baptized Jesus (Jn 1:32, 34). He had watched the Holy Spirit descend from heaven and remain on Him. And based on the language John used, what he saw was not a vision that could be seen only with his spiritual eyes. He indicates that he actually observed the coming of the Spirit with his physical eyes and that the experience was so real it left no doubt in his mind (Mt 3:16; Mk 1:10; Lk 3:21-22; Jn 1:32-34). He said he saw the Holy Spirit come down from heaven like a dove and settle on Jesus (Lk 3:22), and that God had told him that the person upon whom he saw the Spirit rest would perform a ministry similar to his own. He too would baptize people, but instead of immersing them in water as John had, He would baptize them with the Holy Spirit. On another occasion when John was again speaking about Jesus, he added this wonderful insight: "… He whom God has sent speaks the words of God; for He gives the Spirit without measure" (Jn 3:34).

The fourth and final statement John made when he introduced Jesus that day was this: "I myself have seen, and have testified that this is the Son of God" (Jn 1:34). The term "Son of God" was used in Israel as one of the titles for the Messiah (Ps 2:7; Mt 26:63), but when he had baptized Jesus, John had audibly heard the voice of the Father say, "This is My beloved Son, in whom I am well-pleased" (Mt 3:17). And in light of John's earlier statement, that Jesus (who was six months younger than John; see Lk 1:24-27) existed before him (Jn 1:30), John's use of the term "Son of God" must be pointing to the fact that he understood Jesus to be more than a human whom God was choosing to adopt into a son-like relationship. He understood Him to be the only-begotten Son who came from heaven and who fully shares His Father's divine nature (Jn 1:14, 18).

So let's rehearse what we've heard John say about Jesus. He said He is the Lamb of God who takes away our sins. He said He is the pre existent One who came to us from eternity (see also: Jn 3:31-32). He said He is the Baptizer with the Holy Spirit. And he said He is the begotten Son of God.

Believing John

So those four truths are absolutely foundational. And as you would expect each one has been the subject of much debate, and those debates have left a cloud of confusion in the minds of many about who Jesus really is. Sadly some have responded to this confusion by simply avoiding the topic. They prefer to focus on topics where there is general agreement. And there are topics of less importance where that would be a wise course. But understanding Jesus is not such a topic. It is of utmost importance. And if God prepared a man to introduce Jesus to us, then what that man said about Him cannot be ignored. In fact, the four truths he taught are the ones we must proclaim above all others. That's why when we tell people about Jesus:

> First, we must tell them that He is the Lamb of God who takes away their sins by His death on the cross. To ignore that truth or replace it with other teachings is to deny people salvation.
>
> Second, we must tell people that He is the pre-existent One who came to us from eternity. Jesus was not just a prophet. He was not just a great teacher. He was not merely a martyr or tragic victim. He is the divine Son who chose to leave the glories of heaven and become a man. He went willingly to the cross because He was the only One whose death could pay for the sins of the world. If we deny His divinity and pre-existence, we deny the very heart of God's plan to rescue all of us. We deny the reason His death has the power to save us.
>
> Third, we must tell others that Jesus is the Baptizer with the Holy Spirit. This is not a truth that belongs to one group of Christians and not another. It's not an optional benefit for those who are highly emotional. When John introduced Jesus as "the One who baptizes with the Holy Spirit," he was not announcing something new. He was repeating a promise that had been made many times in the Bible. Over the centuries the prophets had declared that the Messiah would do many wonderful things when He came including delivering God's people from oppression, gathering those who were scattered back to the land of Israel, transforming hearts to love and obey God and governing the earth with righteousness. But one of the greatest promises of all was that He would inaugurate the era of the Spirit. When Messiah came, God's presence would come to dwell within His people and would surround His people. They would literally be immersed, "baptized," with the glory of God.
>
> And fourth, we must tell people that Jesus is the begotten Son of God. Like the Father, He is to be worshiped. He is to be obeyed. He is the Lord into whose hands the Father has given all things (Jn 3:35). And when He speaks, His words aren't like

the words we hear from other men. Because He is the Son of God and has come to earth from heaven, when He teaches us about God, He is not telling us what He thinks might be true. He is reporting what He has personally seen and heard (Jn 3:31-32).

Response

Today many voices are saying many different things about Jesus, but we must not allow the confusion they create to cause us to back away from these four, essential truths about Him. We must believe John the Baptist, study his words and then learn to live in the power of what God chose to reveal through him. And then we must proclaim those truths to others. Let's practice:

- Jesus is the Lamb of God who takes away the sin of the world!
- Jesus is the pre-existent One who came from heaven to become a man!
- Jesus is the Baptizer with the Holy Spirit. He has made it possible for the Holy Spirit to live inside us!
- Jesus is the Son of God, so we are to worship, obey and love Him just as we worship, obey and love our heavenly Father and the Holy Spirit!

Chapter Four

The Spirit Arrives

Acts 2:1-21, 37-39

The fulfillment of what Jesus called the Promise of the Father arrived on the day of Pentecost, not when He breathed on His disciples and said, "Receive the Holy Spirit" (Jn 20:22). That symbolic act on the evening of His resurrection identified Him as the One through whom the promised Spirit would soon be given. This is made evident by the fact that just before He ascended into heaven, He said, "And behold, I am sending forth the promise of My Father upon you; but you are to stay in the city until you are clothed with power from on high" (Lk 24:49). Obviously, He did not think the promise had arrived yet. Its arrival would be dramatic!

For centuries the prophets had promised that a day would come when the Holy Spirit would dwell within God's people, and just before He ascended into heaven, Jesus told His disciples to wait in Jerusalem for the fulfillment of that promise. Then ten days later it arrived. A group of about one hundred and twenty men, women and probably children had been gathering daily under a shelter erected on a rooftop in the old city of David. They were waiting for the arrival of that gift by devoting themselves to prayer, and in the book of Acts Luke describes the moment it came. He says it happened at the end of the seven weeks that each year lead up to the Feast of Pentecost (Shavuot) on the morning of the fiftieth day. On that national day of celebration this group of believers in Jesus had already gathered together for prayer in the early hours of the morning when suddenly they heard a sound from heaven which seemed to be moving toward them as if it were being carried on a strong gust of wind. And when that sound reached them, it surrounded them and filled the whole house where they were sitting.

Some students of the Bible have suggested that the "house" in which they were sitting was the temple itself because the temple in Jerusalem can be called the "house of God." But they could not have been inside the temple at that time of the morning because the gates of the temple did not open to the public until the priests finished preparing for the morning offering. Only after everything was ready, and the sacrificial lamb was in place, at about nine o'clock three blasts were sounded on a silver trumpet, and the great doors swung open to invite worshipers to enter (Alfred Edersheim, The Temple, Eerdmans, reprint 1988, p.161). Since Luke tells us that Peter didn't stand up until nine o'clock to preach to the huge crowd that had assembled when they heard the disciples speaking in tongues (Ac 2:15), the actual arrival of the Spirit must have taken place while the temple doors were still closed.

In the second chapter of Acts Luke is describing a very remarkable, spiritual experience, and after carefully studying the original words he chose, here is what seems to have taken place: As the disciples were sitting in an upper room during a time of prayer and praise, which probably included reading or reciting from the Scriptures, everyone, at the same time, suddenly heard a sound from heaven that seemed to be coming toward them like a strong gust of wind. And when it reached them, that heavenly sound filled the whole room. We have no way of knowing what they heard, whether it was music, singing, angelic praise or a voice (Ex 19:16, 19; Eze 1:24-25; Lk 2:13; 2Co 12:4; Rev 5:8-14), but Luke seems to be saying they physically felt it arrive like a wind, and then were enveloped by it. Next, they saw a bright light which looked to them like flames of fire. That light then divided itself into smaller portions, and those portions moved about the room until a fiery light hovered above each person (literal: "it sat on each one"). When a portion of light reached someone, Luke says, "...They were filled with the Holy Spirit and began to speak in other languages, just as the Spirit gave them to speak out" (Ac 2:4, literal).

All through His ministry Jesus had promised that after He ascended into heaven, He would send the Holy Spirit to live inside His disciples (Jn 14:17), and that Pentecost morning was the moment when His promise was fulfilled for the first time. It was the beginning of a new era in the relationship between God's Spirit and His people. Never before had the Holy Spirit been able to inhabit the sin-contaminated bodies of human beings even though God forgave the sins of those who repented and called on Him for mercy. Before Jesus came into the world, the Holy Spirit was able to be with God's people, in some cases at remarkably intense levels (Ex 40:34-35; Nu 11:25; 1Sa 10:1-11; 2Ch 7:1-3), but never before had He been able to dwell in them because their physical bodies were still "unclean." Human flesh is not normally a suitable place for the Holy Spirit to take up residence because the members of our bodies have been used as instruments of sin. But the fact that Jesus was joined to our sinful human flesh at the incarnation means that His death on the cross cleansed not only our human spirit but our sinful flesh as well (Ro 8:3-4, 9-11). It means that though our human body is still subject to disease and death, when we are joined to Christ by faith, our body becomes a suitable place for God to dwell. This explains why it was only after Jesus rose from the dead that this inner baptism could be given. So Luke's account of the day of Pentecost describes a major turning point in the spiritual history of the human race. He allows us to watch as the Ascended Christ for the first time bestows on His people, not the gift of forgiveness, but the gift of the indwelling Spirit. And from that moment on the Holy Spirit has been able to provide believers with the power to walk in genuine holiness (Ro 8:10-13) and to minister as Jesus ministered (Jn 14:12; Ac 1:8).

Speaking in tongues

When that first infilling took place, a remarkable manifestation occurred. Every one of those disciples began to speak in a language that he or she had never learned. Luke says they spoke words that the Spirit gave them to speak, and there is no record of a miracle like that ever taking place before that moment. There are numerous examples over the course of Israel's history of the Holy Spirit coming upon people to enable them to prophesy in their own language, but never before was anyone enabled to speak in an unlearned language. Yet when we read through the book of Acts, we discover that what happened on the day of Pentecost was not an isolated miracle. Luke specifically records that people spoke in tongues, or indirectly refers to speaking in tongues, several more times. Apparently it happened when Peter and John laid their hands on Philip the Evangelist's converts in Samaria (Ac 8:12-18). It is reasonable to assume that it happened when Ananias laid his hands on Paul in Damascus (Ac 9:17; 1Co 14:18). Luke specifically says it happened when Peter preached to the household of a Roman centurion named Cornelius (Ac 10:44-48; 11:15-18), and he also says twelve disciples of Apollos spoke in tongues and prophesied when Paul laid his hands on them in the city of Ephesus, and that miracle happened twenty-six years after that original outpouring on the day of Pentecost (Ac 19:1-6).

Peter's announcement

Each year on the day before the Feast of Pentecost, tens of thousands of pilgrims would enter the city of Jerusalem. And when the first stars appeared in the evening sky, priests in the temple would sound silver trumpets to announce that the feast had officially begun. The special offerings that the people presented to the Lord at that feast included two loaves of leavened bread made from wheat flour, and two, year-old lambs, one for a sin offering and the other for a peace (or fellowship) offering (Josephus, Antiquities, 3.10.6; 17.10.2; Alfred Edersheim, The Temple, Eerdmans reprint 1988, pp.262-263). Then, shortly after midnight the temple gates would be opened to allow worshipers to show their sacrificial animals to the priests so they could inspect them by lamplight to ensure that they were without blemish. Many priests were kept hard at work conducting those inspections all through the night, but as morning approached, a priest stationed at the southeast corner of the temple would watch for the moment when the sun's first rays touched the mountains of Hebron nineteen miles to the south. That would be the signal for everyone to leave the temple and the gates to be closed so preparations could begin for the regular morning sacrifice which was performed at around nine o'clock ("the third hour") (Alfred Edersheim, The Temple, Eerdmans, reprint 1988, p.161). When the sacrificial animal was ready, the gates would be re-opened and three blasts would be sounded on silver trumpets to call the nation to worship (Nu 10:2, 10). The waiting multitude would then surge through the city streets and into the temple. But on the Day of Pentecost that Luke describes, as that multitude was moving toward the temple, the sound of a hundred and twenty or more voices could be heard speaking in foreign languages on a nearby rooftop.

And it's no surprise that the roar of all those voices caught the attention of passing pilgrims and drew many of them toward the house where the disciples were gathered. But the narrow streets in that part of the city were not a satisfactory place to address such a large crowd, so at some point the disciples must have moved to a location where everyone could hear them. And the most likely site for that was only a short distance away. It was the broad, southern steps that led up into the temple. In effect those steps formed an amphitheater where thousands of people could sit and listen as Peter and the Eleven spoke.

Luke says, "And standing with the Eleven, Peter lifted up his voice and declared, 'Men, Jews and all those living in Jerusalem, let this be known to you, and listen to my words, for these are not drunk as was mistakenly reported to you, for it is the third hour of the day [9 a.m.]. But this is that which was spoken through the prophet Joel'" (Ac 2:14-16, literal). In other words, Peter was telling them that he was about to answer the question in everyone's mind: "What does this mean?" (Ac 2:12). And the answer he gave to the crowd that day was stunning. He said that the "last days" outpouring of the Holy Spirit which the prophet Joel describes in his writings had begun that morning. He explained that the transformation of ordinary people into prophets, which was taking place in front of their very eyes, was not only like the miracle Joel said would happen at the end of the age, it was the actual beginning of that miracle. Basically he announced that because the Messiah had come, from the perspective of God's timetable, the world had now moved into the "last days". Yes, the Messiah had come in a way that most of Israel did not recognize, but that was because their teachers had not fully understood the Scriptures. But the indisputable proof that Jesus was the Messiah was that He had been resurrected from the dead. And now, seated at the right hand of God, He was pouring out the Holy Spirit on all who believed in Him. Though many of the events that the Bible says will take place at the end of the age had not yet happened, Peter declared to that crowd that the Messiah had already begun saving anyone who would call on His name and doing what Joel said He would do: He was pouring out the Holy Spirit on men and women, and they were speaking prophetically by the power of God. And then Peter invited those who were listening to repent and declare their faith in Jesus by being baptized in His name, and he assured them that "Jesus will forgive your sins and give you the same gift of the Holy Spirit that He has given to us" (Ac 2:38, paraphrase). And as if he knew that we would still be reading his words centuries later, Peter added this: "For the promise is for you and your children and for all who are far off, as many as the Lord our God will call to Himself" (Ac 2:39).

Conclusion

When Peter preached that sermon, the end of the age had not arrived, and they all knew that. Jesus had made that fact very clear to His disciples before He ascended into heaven (Ac 1:6-7). But the most wonderful part of the "last days" is the arrival of the Messiah, and what Peter told the crowd that day was that the Messiah had indeed come. But instead of bringing history to a close, His arrival had initiated a new season of harvest. He explained to them that God's plan for the "last days" had always included an extended season of evangelism, a great gathering in of souls of both Jews and Gentiles from all over the world. He said the outpouring of the Holy Spirit that they were observing was meant to be a beginning, not an ending. It was the beginning of an extended harvest that will end only when the Father decides it is time (Mt 24:36; Mk 13:32; Ac 1:7).

And today, two thousand years later, the Father hasn't done that yet. He is still saving people. He is still filling them with the Holy Spirit and sending them into the world to win more. The last days' harvest is still going strong because the message Peter spoke at that first Pentecost is still true. Jesus will save all who will call on His name, and the promise of the Holy Spirit will be given to "...as many as the Lord our God will call to Himself." Listen: "Repent, and each of you be baptized in the name of Jesus Christ for the forgiveness of your sins; and you will receive the gift of the Holy Spirit" (Ac 2:38).

Chapter Five

Receiving the Spirit

There are occasions when people are suddenly and unexpectedly baptized with the Holy Spirit, but normally those who receive Jesus Christ as their Lord and Savior need to seek this gift. This lesson is meant to encourage us to pursue what has already been given to us in Christ.

A discussion about receiving the Holy Spirit has been going on in the family of God for a long time. People have been trying to answer a very important question: When does a person receive the baptism with the Holy Spirit? One perspective is that everyone who repents and believes on the Lord Jesus Christ receives the Holy Spirit immediately, and in most cases, imperceptibly. This view expects no unusual phenomena to accompany the arrival of the Spirit, but firmly relies on the promises in the Bible that state that the Holy Spirit will be given to every believer. And we need look no further for such promises than Jesus' statement to His disciples in the upper room before He was arrested: "I will ask the Father, and He will give you another Helper, that He may be with you forever" (Jn 14:16); or Peter's sermon on Pentecost which he concluded by saying, "Repent, and each of you be baptized in the name of Jesus Christ for the forgiveness of your sins, and you will receive the gift of the Holy Spirit" (Ac 2:38-39). Nothing in Jesus' or Peter's statements suggests that a person who repents and believes might not be given the Holy Spirit. So whether or not there is any noticeable evidence of the Spirit's indwelling, based on God's promises, we can be confident that He has come.

Another perspective turns to the book of Acts and observes that every time the Holy Spirit baptized a person or a group of people there was visible evidence of His power coming upon them, and that evidence included miraculous speech, either speaking in tongues or prophecy. This view also observes that the reception of this gift did not always occur right away. For example, in Samaria water-baptized believers had to wait until Peter and John arrived and laid their hands on them before they received the baptism with the Holy Spirit with visible evidence (Ac 8:15-17). The apostle Paul was powerfully converted by a direct encounter with the risen Jesus on the road to Damascus, but he didn't receive the baptism with the Holy Spirit until Ananias laid his hands on him three days later and prayed that he be "filled with the Holy Spirit" (Ac 9:17). Yet those in Cornelius' household did not have to wait. They received the moment they believed. The Spirit's power fell on them, and they immediately began to speak in tongues and exalt God (Ac 10:44-48). Many years later, when Paul encountered a group of disciples in Ephesus whom Apollos had led to repentance and faith in Jesus (Ac 18:24-25), he asked them this question: "Did you receive the Holy Spirit when you believed?" And they replied, "No, we have not even heard whether there is a Holy Spirit" (Ac 19:2). Then after baptizing them in water again to allow them to fully express their faith in Jesus' death and resurrection, Paul laid his hands on them and prayed for them to receive the Holy Spirit, and they spoke with tongues and prophesied (Ac 19:5-6). So a review of the book of Acts teaches us that the baptism with the Holy Spirit is not necessarily automatic, nor is it imperceptible when it is received. In fact, it's a gift that may need to be sought for, and when it occurs, it will be miraculously confirmed. In particular, those who have been baptized with the Holy Spirit will be able to speak in tongues or prophesy.

The perspective that says a person is always given the baptism with the Holy Spirit when he or she believes has strong promises to stand on. But the perspective that says that the baptism with the Holy Spirit is a transformative power that can be felt and observed, and will produce active gifts of the Spirit when it arrives, in particular speaking in tongues, also has strong, biblical examples to stand on. So let's try to understand the truth that each of these perspectives presents so that by believing <u>both</u> truths we can receive and minister the Holy Spirit just as Jesus promised and the book of Acts reveals.

All things (1Co 3:21-23)

In writing to the church in Corinth Paul made a remarkable statement while he was correcting a wrong attitude that had been dividing the congregation into factions. People were separating themselves into groups based on who they considered to be their leader. Some chose Paul, some Apollos, some Peter (Cephas) and some Jesus (1Co 1:12). But since Paul had originally founded the church in Corinth, the only reason for choosing another leader was to announce that Paul was not their leader. And certain individuals had been undermining his authority by criticizing his appearance and speaking ability and even the fact that he didn't collect financial offerings to support his ministry. But Paul identified the real reason they were attacking him in his response to those charges. He said they were turning away from his gospel. The cross and resurrection that he had preached to them now seemed foolish. The gospel was causing them to be persecuted, and it didn't make sense to their logical minds. So Paul warned them of what would happen if they left the gospel. And in that warning he reminded them that he, and those they had named as their leaders, served the same Lord and would answer to Him for what they taught. Then in the midst of that warning, he made a statement that is so amazing we need to stop and read it several times to grasp its meaning. Listen:

> "So then let no one boast in men. For all things belong to you, whether Paul or Apollos or Cephas or the world or life or death or things present or things to come; all things belong to you, and you belong to Christ; and Christ belongs to God" (1Co 3:21-23).

He said <u>all things</u> belonged to them. And in case anyone missed his point he elaborated on what he meant by "all things," and that list included: the world, life, death, things present and things to come. In other words, he was trying to show them what it means to be "heirs of God and fellow heirs with Christ" (Ro 8:17). He wanted them to understand the implications of a very important spiritual truth: that everything that the Father has given to His Son, Jesus, has also been given to those who believe in Jesus. To be joined to God's Son by faith means we have entered into a spiritual union with Him which is like the marriage of a man and woman. But instead of each partner in that marriage owning only half the estate, as might be true in an earthly marriage, in Christ both partners own all of the estate. So those who are "married" to Jesus have inherited with Him every good thing the Father gave His Son. As Paul says elsewhere: "He who did not spare His own Son, but delivered Him over for us all, how will He not also with Him freely give us all things?" (Ro 8:32).

So here's how this amazing truth applies to the subject of the baptism of the Holy Spirit. When we are joined by faith to Jesus Christ, a genuine spiritual union takes place. And when that happens, God gives us every good gift that belongs to His Son, and those good gifts certainly include the baptism with the Holy Spirit. Jesus Himself was baptized with the Holy Spirit, and He is the Baptizer with the Holy Spirit, so when you or I belong to Him, that gift always, immediately and unreservedly is given to us. The righteousness Jesus won for us by His crucifixion and resurrection is all the qualification we need. No higher qualification is possible. That means that a person who genuinely repents and places their faith in Him need never wonder if the Holy Spirit was given to them when they believed. Of course He was. Yet it's also apparent that not everyone who believes in Jesus receives that full measure of power. And that brings us to the second perspective that says the baptism with the Holy Spirit is a transformative power that must be actively received by faith.

Receiving what God has given

This perspective teaches us that to actually possess God's gifts, we need to reach out by faith and take hold of them, and that by not understanding that fact, many people are prevented from enjoying the blessings God wants to give them, including the baptism with the Holy Spirit. The following insight will help us understand the part we humans must play in the process: Receiving the baptism with the Holy Spirit involves two participants. First, there is God who gives the Spirit, and second, there is the human who receives the Spirit. And much of the confusion that surrounds this subject arises when we don't recognize both sides of the process. We must realize that there is a divine side and a human side, and that what God gives must be actively received. We must not make the mistake of assuming that if God wants us to receive this "baptism," it will simply appear automatically, that we don't need to do anything to get it. Or that if someone has asked for this blessing but doesn't appear to have received it, that must mean God doesn't want him or her to have it. A brief review of the Bible will prove that those assumptions are wrong because it's full of examples of people who didn't receive what God wanted to give them, not because He wasn't willing to give it, but because they wouldn't step out by faith and take hold of what He had promised. And the lesson we learn from their failure is that we humans must not be passive when it comes to receiving God's promised blessings. To better understand this truth, let's listen to how Jesus pictures the process of God giving and our receiving the baptism with the Holy Spirit:

> "Everyone who drinks of this water [Jacob's well] will thirst again; but whoever drinks of the water that I will give him shall never thirst; but the water that I will give him will become in him a well of water springing up to eternal life" (Jn 4:13-14).

> "If anyone is thirsty, let him come to Me and drink. He who believes in Me, as the Scriptures said, 'From his innermost being will flow rivers of living water'" (Jn 7:37-38).

If we observe both of these statements carefully, we will recognize that there are two active participants in the process of someone being baptized with the Holy Spirit: Jesus, who pours out the "water," and the thirsty person who must drink it. In other words, Jesus gives the Spirit, but it's our responsibility to receive the Spirit. Jesus used a similar illustration when He breathed on His disciples and said, "Receive the Holy Spirit" (Jn 20:22): He breathes out the Holy Spirit, but we must breathe Him in. His part then is to send the Holy Spirit to us, which, as we saw earlier, He does as soon as we believe in Him. He gives all of the Holy Spirit (Jn 3:34) to every believer as soon as they believe. But as we have also seen, that doesn't mean every believer has actively reached out by faith and taken hold of this deep, indwelling, transformative power. If someone is not taught to expect it, or is not provided the pastoral help they might need at the moment, or has been taught that the gifts of the Spirit are no longer available to us today as they were in Bible times, then Jesus can give the baptism with the Holy Spirit to that person in potential, but it might go unreceived in practice.

Conclusion

The baptism with the Holy Spirit is not meant to be a theological truth we affirm but never experience. God intended it to be a very real encounter with His power. And as we've seen in the book of Acts, and possibly in our own practical experience, the reception of this power is not necessarily automatic. We may need to pursue it. But as we also learned from the book of Acts, when it arrives, we will know it. It's simply impossible for the Creator of heaven and earth to fill us with His power and for us to be unaware of it. We may not be able to explain what happened to us, but we know that we have been changed; we will know that God is real and that He now dwells inside us. And as we will learn in the next chapter, when we receive this baptism with the Holy Spirit, we will also discover that we are able to speak in tongues and prophesy.

Chapter Six

Giving God Our Tongue

Acts 2:1-21

The fear of speaking in tongues can be a barrier that prevents people from receiving the baptism with the Holy Spirit. And that fear may arise because of a misunderstanding of what actually occurs when someone speaks in tongues. Yet as we'll see in this lesson, the Lord asks us to give Him the control of our tongue for very important reasons. Understanding why the Lord asks us to take this step can help us overcome this fear and enjoy the blessings this gift will bring.

When the Spirit arrived on the day of Pentecost, a miracle took place that involved the human tongue. An entire group of people, possibly a hundred and twenty men, women and even children, began to speak in languages that they had never learned. Luke explains that the Holy Spirit gave them those words to speak. Never before had there been such a miracle in Israel's history. There had been numerous occasions when the Spirit came upon people, and they prophesied in their own language (Nu 11:24-26; 1Sa 10:5-13; 19:20-24; 2Ki 3:15; 1Ch 12:18; 25:1-6; 2Ch 15:1-7; 24:20; Eze 2:2; 11:4-5; Zec 7:12). But there is no record of anyone being enabled to speak in a foreign language.

The disciples were gathered under a covered area on a rooftop in Jerusalem, so when they all began to speak in new languages, the sound of their voices could be heard by pilgrims walking through the surrounding streets on their way to the temple. And based on the way Luke reports this event, what each of those pilgrims heard also involved a miracle. He carefully chose his words to explain that each listener heard all one hundred and twenty voices speaking in his or her native language. The pilgrims filling the streets that day came from many different nations. They were there to celebrate the Feast of Pentecost, and though some of them would have known Hebrew, and most would have known Greek, each one would also have spoken a local dialect from the region in which they were born. Yet on that day every one of them miraculously understood everything being said by those speaking in tongues because they all heard the disciples speaking in their own dialect. So there were actually two miracles that morning. First, the Holy Spirit gave each disciple a new language, and second, He gave each listener the ability to understand what was said because they heard the disciples speaking in the language that they spoke at home. And what they heard the disciples saying was praise. They heard them declaring the mighty deeds of God (Ac 2:11).

Many suggestions have been offered to explain what happened that day. Some have called it "ecstatic" speech, meaning that the disciples were in such an emotional frenzy that they compulsively blurted out gibberish. There were people at the time who mockingly suggested the disciples were drunk (Ac 2:13), though as we've seen, their speech was not garbled but was understood by all. And some have suggested that God momentarily gave the disciples the ability to preach the gospel in the different languages spoken by that diverse crowd. But none of these suggestions takes into account Peter's own explanation. He said they weren't drunk, and what they were saying wasn't gibberish. He said it was a form of prophecy. He said it was a sign that the spiritual restoration of Israel, which the prophets had said would come before the final battle of the last days, had begun (Ac 2:14-21).

Those who say that the speaking in tongues that happened that day was only a momentary miracle designed to evangelize that diverse crowd overlook the fact that Peter went on to evangelize that same crowd using only one language, probably Greek. Then as now, the people who lived in that part of the world spoke numerous languages. And in every age there is always one particular language in a region that is used in commerce. It's the language people use when conducting business or speaking to a diverse group, and at that point in time and in that region of the world, the language of commerce was Greek. The book of Acts preserves the basic outline of the sermon Peter preached that day, and it was pure evangelism. He proclaimed the death and resurrection of Jesus, and then called on his listeners to repent and be baptized. And he didn't need interpreters to translate what he said because one language was enough. Everyone understood what he was saying. So the miracle of speaking in tongues was not given to those disciples to preach the gospel to that crowd. Instead it was a gift God gave them to equip them for the ministry that lay ahead. Jesus was preparing His "prophets" for the last days, and Peter said He will continue to offer that same gift to everyone who believes until "the great and glorious day of the Lord shall come" (Ac 2:20). So let's try to understand why God would want all of us to speak in tongues.

Understanding the gift

What is speaking in tongues? It is a spiritual gift that allows our human spirit to speak directly to God using words we have never learned. Words that didn't originate in our minds flow out of our lips, and though we don't understand what we're saying, God does. And He is pleased with what He hears because the Holy Spirit is guiding us to say the very things we would have said if we were wise enough, good enough or brave enough to have thought of them and been willing to say them. According to the Bible, when we speak in tongues we may be telling Him we love Him more intensely than we would normally allow ourselves to say it, or we may be surrendering more deeply than "common sense" would allow us to do, or we may be interceding for people and situations our distracted minds had forgotten.

Paul says this gift of language is a great help to us personally and to the church corporately because through speaking in tongues the Spirit is able to guide us to pray rightly. We are not left in our weakness to struggle to know what to say, but we can pray in such a way that allows us to receive God's strength (Ro 8:26). And we are also able to worship supernaturally, and that helps us to be filled afresh with His presence and for our hearts to be lifted when we are sad. By praying and worshiping in the Spirit we are able to find God's joy at times when we might otherwise have considered medicating our misery in an unhealthy way (Eph 5:18-20). Jude tells us that by speaking in tongues we are able to build ourselves up in our "most holy faith" (Jude 1:20), and Paul says we can use it to refresh a gathering of believers by providing a Spirit-inspired word of praise, thanksgiving or intercession. And in those situations when the Lord asks us to speak in tongues before a gathering of believers, we remember Paul's caution that our words should be interpreted so everyone can understand what we said (1Co 14:5, 26-28).

Overcoming the fear

The idea of speaking words we don't understand, of allowing the Holy Spirit to literally control our tongue, can be very intimidating. Few areas in our personality are more central to who we are, more embedded in our self-identity, than our speech. In fact, it can be difficult for a person to think through a matter without talking. Our words are usually the major way we express ourselves. They are the tools we use to tell others about our joy, sorrow, desire, fear, hope or anger. What we feel or think generally flows out of our mouth in words, so to release the control of our tongue, even to God, involves a profound level of trust. It's both frightening and humbling which is one reason why so many people struggle the first time they are asked to yield their tongue to Him. Other gifts of the Spirit allow the conscious mind to remain active and to filter what we say. They too require us to say things inspired by the Spirit, but only speaking in tongues requires us to completely yield control of what is said to the point that we don't know what we are saying. All we hear are unrecognizable sounds (1Co 14:14).

So if speaking in tongues is that intimidating, why would anyone do it? Why would a rational person take that first step into the unknown and yield control of their tongue to the Holy Spirit? The answer is simple: We desperately need the help this gift is designed to bring us. Every follower of Jesus Christ is called to "walk in the Spirit," which means that sooner or later every one of us must take our first step into the realm of the miraculous. Like Peter stepping out of the boat and discovering that he was able to walk on water (Mt 14:28-29), each of us must learn to trust that God will undergird us when we take that first step of faith into the realm of the miraculous. It seems there is a scary first-time for everybody. And then of course, the Lord requires many more such steps because He has called us to be led by the Spirit and to move freely in all of the gifts of the Spirit. But our walk in the Spirit often begins when we overcome our fear and yield our tongue to God.

The unruly member (Jas 3:1-12)

There is also another important reason that God wants us to yield the control of our tongue to Him. It's found in the book of James. While warning teachers about the judgment they will face if they teach falsely, James explains the profound influence of the tongue. He says that even though it is a very small organ in the human body, it exerts a huge influence on our lives. Just as a horse can be steered by a small bit placed in its mouth, or a great ship can be steered by a small rudder at its stern, he says if a person can control their tongue, they will be able to control the direction of their life. He also notes that it only takes a small flame to start a forest fire, and likewise our tongue can be used by the enemy to set our entire life on fire. He says the tongue, by its nature, is untamable and full of deadly poison, and even believers tend to use it hypocritically. With it we bless God and curse our neighbor. It's a fountain that pours out both fresh and bitter water. So it should come as no surprise that a full surrender to God must include our tongue. We can't give Him everything else but withhold control of that "unruly member." And it's here that speaking in tongues plays such a valuable role. When we trust God enough to allow the Holy Spirit to take our tongue and guide it to speak a new language, when we allow Him to direct our prayer and praise using words we don't understand, we are in effect "stepping out of the boat" and walking in a level of trust that will release us to walk in the other gifts of the Spirit as well.

Receiving this gift

If a person wants to receive the gift of speaking in tongues, he or she might begin by reminding themselves of this important truth: We who believe in Jesus have been spiritually joined to Him and are "co-heirs" with Him, so our heavenly Father has given us every good gift (Ro 8:32; 1Co 3:21-23). That means that when we come to Him to ask for this gift of spiritual language, we don't need to beg Him to give it to us, nor do we need to wonder if He desires to give it to us. Because of Jesus, our Father is pleased to give us everything we need. And here's a great promise that will remind us of that truth:

> "This is the confidence which we have before Him, that, if we ask anything according to His will, He hears us. And if we know that He hears us [in] whatever we ask, we know that we have the requests which we have asked from Him" (1Jn 5:14-15).

It may also be helpful to ask someone who already speaks in tongues to lay hands on us as we begin. But it is not necessary because Jesus is the Baptizer with the Holy Spirit, and He can give us a new language when we are alone. But whether we are alone or not, it's important to spiritually prepare ourselves before we try. The first thing we must do is become aware of the presence of the Holy Spirit. Whether by worship, prayer, quiet meditation or even fasting we need to press through any barriers and welcome His presence to "warm" the room. Then once we sense Him near, we need to speak directly to Him and tell Him that we understand the promise we have been given and that we wish to receive this gift.

And here we need to add a note of caution: When some people sense the Holy Spirit move upon them and start to guide their tongue, they pull back because they are startled by the reality of what they are experiencing. Or they may become troubled because of teachings they had received. Some people were taught that "speaking in tongues is not a gift for today," and they become confused and feel guilty. They know that what is happening is real but were taught that it shouldn't happen, so they may need to stop and take time to study the Scriptures for themselves to satisfy their conscience that this is indeed God's will for them. It is best not to press someone who is struggling this way to ignore their conscience.

If we are not hindered by such fears when we strongly sense His presence, then we should step out by faith and begin to speak something other than our native language. We should not try to mimic what another person is saying, or listen to ourselves and try to analyze our words to determine if we are actually speaking a "real" language or not. Instead we should carefully focus our thoughts on the Lord and the words that come out of our mouth should be spoken directly to Him.

And here is another helpful insight: When we are trying to release our tongue to the Holy Spirit, we shouldn't think that we will be overcome by compulsive speech as if the Spirit will physically take control of our tongue and jaw. We must make the effort to speak. We must try to utter some sort of sound. But at some point as a new language begins, we will find that we no longer have to make an effort to form the words. They seem to arise from our heart and flow out of our mouth. We won't be inventing words in our mind; we will simply be speaking what the Spirit gives us.

Then once we begin to speak in tongues, we need to continue speaking and to carefully enunciate the words we're saying. We should not fall into a pattern of simply repeating the same syllables over and over. If we keep our thoughts focused on Him and keep speaking out, at some point we will sense a flow of language come out of our "innermost being" that we do not have to labor to produce, and we will feel the strengthening of the Spirit's presence. When that happens, it's a good idea to continue on speaking in our new language in order to let our heart worship freely for as long as it wants to. Sometimes God will do a deep healing in us while we're speaking. Then when we sense we have finished saying to God all that our heart needed to say to Him at that moment, we can switch back to our native language and pray again with understanding (1Co 14:15). Even as we do this, if we let thoughts that come from the Spirit guide our words, we will find that we can let Him lead in every form of prayer or worship. By shifting back and forth between praying in the Spirit and praying with understanding, we will quickly discover that we can speak in tongues whenever we want to. We will learn that we can awaken our spiritual senses when the need arises and to be led by the Spirit. And that is a very important lesson. It will release us to step out in the other spoken gifts as well, such as prophecy, the word of knowledge, the word of wisdom and interpretation of tongues because we have learned to give our tongue to God.

Chapter Seven

Helping Others Receive the Gift of Tongues

People often need someone to help them receive the gift of speaking in tongues, and God may ask you to minister in this way. Here is a simple, step-by-step outline designed to help you help others.

There is no formula by which a person can cause someone else to speak in tongues, but many people do need some level of personal help when it comes to receiving this gift. What follows are seven steps that often need to be considered when helping someone who desires to speak in tongues:

1. Assess where the person is spiritually. Are they saved, and if so, for how long? Have they already had a powerful encounter with God? Were they permanently changed by that encounter? What have they been taught about speaking in tongues if anything? Do they understand the purpose of tongues? Is the power of the Holy Spirit present at that moment? If not, it would be best to worship and praise freely until the atmosphere changes. Is there any physical evidence that the Spirit has already begun to move upon this person (weeping, trembling, weakness, excitement, joy, a consciousness of God's presence, unusual freedom in worship or prayer, spontaneous confession of sin, etc.)? Does he or she need to be baptized with the Holy Spirit, or has that event already happened, and what they need from you is merely help to receive tongues?

2. Explain that speaking in tongues is inspired speech, not compulsive speech. Tell them that they must actively engage their tongue, lips, breath, etc. If they will begin to make sounds, the Spirit will form those sounds into words to speak. Those words seem to rise up from the "belly"; they are not invented in the mind.

3. Explain, "Here's what we're going to do":

   - We'll pray, specifically thanking God for giving you this gift when you received Jesus as your Lord and Savior, and then we will ask Him to help you receive what already belongs to you.

   - Ask, "May I lay my hand (or hands) on your forehead or the back of your head?" Ask permission before you do this, and if they prefer that you not, remember that it is not necessary to lay on hands since Jesus is the Baptizer with the Holy Spirit. It is often helpful to do so, but it is not essential.

   - Tell them, "I'm going to begin speaking in tongues loud enough to give you some privacy, and then I would like you to place your thoughts on Jesus and speak to Him, not in our own language but with those words that will well up from within you."

   - Explain that they need to be willing to make sounds that aren't words they recognize. At some point if they will take that step, they'll sense a flow of words being given to them by the Holy Spirit.

   - Do not ask them to mimic what you are saying. Do not suggest that they repeat a nonsense phrase to get them started. Assure them that God will provide them with their own language(s). If we manipulate a person into saying something that is self-generated, they will lose the joy of their encounter and later question the reality of this gift.

4. Listen to their progress:

   - If the person has begun to speak in tongues, encourage the person to enunciate those words and speak them out boldly.

- If the person is not able to speak, listen for the Spirit's instructions. He may give you a "word of knowledge" or some other prophetic insight to reveal what is obstructing the person's progress.
- If they have remained silent, encourage them to step out and try, but assure them that you are not evaluating them, and there is no need to perform for you. You are only there to help.
- Ask, "What's happening? Do you sense that God is doing something?"
- If you believe the Lord has shown you an obstacle, share it humbly and then ask them if what you've said is helpful. If not, move on.
- Ask, "Would you like to continue trying?" If not, remind them that God can meet them when they are alone just as well.
- Assure them that their inability to speak yet does not indicate that they are not fit to receive. God is not withholding this gift; they are simply learning how to receive it.
- Pray for the Lord to continue the work He has begun in them.
- Assure them that you, or someone else, will be available again, if needed, and that you are prepared to walk with them through this process until they finally are able to speak in tongues.

5. Encourage the person who has begun speaking in tongues to continue speaking for a while. Let them freely pour out their heart to God. There is often some form of inner healing going on. Be sensitive not to intrude if they are having a deep encounter, but when the time seems right, ask them to switch back to their own language and praise God with understanding. Then after a brief season of free praise, ask them to return to tongues, so they learn by experience that they can access this gift whenever they wish. Move from one to the other several times.

6. Encourage the person to speak in tongues and even sing in tongues (1Co 14:15) when they have a private moment later that day, and to continue doing so each day until it becomes a beautiful part of their pattern of worship and prayer.

7. Thank God together for His faithfulness.

Conclusion

Once a person has been baptized with the Holy Spirit and has learned to pray and praise as the Spirit gives them "utterance" (Ac 2:4), the next lesson he or she needs to learn is how to "be filled with the Spirit" (Eph 5:18) over and over again. The baptism with the Holy Spirit is the moment when the Spirit indwells, and the believer's body becomes the tabernacle of God, but those who are indwelt by the Spirit still need to learn how to receive fresh outpourings of His presence; they need to know where to find protection when attacks come and how to be strengthened when they are weak. Their success and fruitfulness will depend on it.

Chapter Eight

The Perfect and the Partial

1 Corinthians 13:8-12

There are those who have been taught that the supernatural gifts of the Spirit, including speaking in tongues, are not meant for today. And that misunderstanding can become an obstacle that prevents them from receiving the baptism with the Holy Spirit. Here is a discussion of a key verse of Scripture which is often used to argue that these gifts passed away when the canon of the Bible was complete. What we discover when we look closely at this verse is that it actually assures us that the gifts of the Spirit will be given to believers until Jesus comes again.

There are sincere, Bible-believing Christians who have been taught that the gifts of the Holy Spirit such as prophecy, speaking in tongues and the word of knowledge were only meant for the early church. The idea behind this teaching is that God chose to perform such miracles during the first decades of the church's existence because the New Testament had not yet been written. Because those first-century disciples did not have a complete Bible, God needed to speak to them directly. And He sent special miracles to confirm His choice of the apostles and the truth of the gospel they preached. But according to this teaching, once the New Testament was complete, and there is still much discussion as to when that moment arrived, these "sign gifts" were no longer needed, and God stopped speaking to His people in that way. From that point on believers were to hear Him speak only through His written Word. The passage of Scripture which is most often quoted in support of this theory is the following:

> "Love never fails; but if there are gifts of prophecy, they will be done away; if there are tongues, they will cease; if there is knowledge, it will be done away. For we know in part and we prophesy in part; but when the perfect comes, the partial will be done away. When I was a child, I used to speak like a child, think like a child, reason like a child; when I became a man, I did away with childish things. For now we see in a mirror dimly, but then face to face; now I know in part, but then I will know fully just as I also have been fully known" (1Co 13:8-12).

In order for this passage to mean that Paul expected the gifts of the Spirit such as prophecy, tongues and the word of knowledge to pass away when the New Testament was written, the Greek word which is translated here as "the perfect," must be understood to mean the completed Bible containing both Old and New Testaments. Those who believe this theory, which is often called "cessationism," also believe that Paul calls prophecy, tongues and the revelational gifts, such as the word of knowledge, "the partial" because they are imperfect substitutes compared to the perfect revelation of truth found in Scripture. And for that reason cessationism teaches that they were only meant to be used by the church until the last book of the New Testament was written. At that point God stopped giving those gifts to anyone because they were incomplete. They were like a child's understanding of things when compared to the full revelation of Scripture. They were so limited that they were like looking into an ancient mirror made of polished metal. What they presented was indistinct and blurred compared to the clear, face-to-face revelation of the written documents. And based on that assumption, that God stopped speaking through those gifts after the Bible was completed, the only possible conclusion which can be drawn about any prophecies, gifts of tongues or words of knowledge which are spoken today is that they cannot possibly be from God because He stopped speaking that way nearly 2,000 years ago. So according to that theory, anything we hear today is at best human-generated thoughts or at worst demonic utterances.

Since this theory of cessationism is widely taught in certain areas of the church, and since this passage is central to that teaching, it is important for us to study what Paul wrote to the Corinthian church to see if indeed that was his meaning. If it was, then all attempts to minister in the miraculous or spoken gifts of the Spirit should be stopped immediately. But if that is not his meaning, then we must answer the question, "What did he mean?" And to do that we must discover two things: What is the "perfect," and why will it cause the "partial" to be done away?

The Corinthian church

One of the main problems Paul observed in the church at Corinth was that many of its members used the gifts of the Holy Spirit selfishly. They operated in God's power but weren't guided by love. Paul opened his letter to them by acknowledging "that in everything you were enriched in Him, in all speech and all knowledge... so that you are not lacking in any gift..." (1Co 1:5-7). He meant by that statement that a large percentage of the church was functioning freely in various forms of prophetic speech and knowledge. But as his letter goes on to reveal, their character development had not kept up with their giftedness. They were divided, proud and tolerant of flagrant immorality. Some had even returned to idol temples and apparently were participating in the sacred meals and ritual prostitution that was part of the worship of the goddess Aphrodite. But in Paul's mind one of their greatest failures was their lovelessness because it spoiled everything they did for God. It had ruined their communion services (bread and cup) to the point that some of them had fallen under severe judgment. It had soured their church gatherings to the point that Paul considered them to be more damaging than helpful. He said people were coming to church only to get a blessing for themselves, not to minister to others, and they were certainly not interested in caring for the needs of their unsaved guests or the new believers who were present. So Paul devoted several chapters of this letter to show them how God viewed their loveless attitude and to explain how the gifts of the Spirit should operate when they are used properly. Chapter thirteen is often called "the love chapter," and it is indeed one of the most beautiful statements ever made about love. But it was never meant to stand alone. It is an integral part of Paul's correction of this loveless church. He wrote it to explain what real love, God's kind of love, looks like because he was dealing with a group of people who clearly didn't know. He wrote it to show them how unloving they had become and to warn them of what would happen when Jesus returns. He explained that all the gifts will disappear because they won't be needed anymore, and then when Jesus personally examines each of our lives, the quality He will look for above all others is love, real love, selfless love... just like His.

The perfect (1Cor 13:10-12)

The Greek word in this verse which is translated as "the perfect" is teleios. It usually refers to something that has gone through various stages of development and has arrived at its goal. It has become mature, complete, fully grown; it has reached the ideal. The word can be applied to people or things (He 9:11; 1Jn 4:18). For example, it might describe a building that has passed through different phases of construction and is finally complete. It might refer to the final stage of a rose which has grown from a green bud into a beautiful flower. It might picture a human being who has passed from childhood to adulthood. And it is often used in the Bible to point to someone who has reached spiritual maturity (Mt 5:48; 19:21; 1Co 14:20; Eph 4:13; Col 1:28; He 5:14; Jas 1:4). He or she has become the person God wanted him or her to become; nothing is missing, and nothing is undeveloped.

So in this verse Paul is telling us that we are waiting for something or someone who is mature, complete and has reached God's ideal. And all doubt about what or to whom he's referring disappears when we read verse twelve. Let's hear it again:

> "For we still see through a mirror dimly [Greek: ainigma (in prophetic utterances and visions; see G. Kittle, Theological Dictionary of the New Testament, Eerdmans, one volume, "ainigma" p.27, 1985)] but then face to face; I still know in part, but then I shall fully know just as I was fully known" (1Co 13:12, literal).

When Paul speaks of being "face to face," and says we shall "fully know" God just as we are now "fully known" by Him, he can only be talking about the return of Jesus Christ and the fact that when He comes, He will bring the kingdom of God to earth. There is no place in all of Scripture where the term teleios means the Bible, and the Bible never uses the words "the perfect" to refer to itself. So a proper understanding of what Paul says in this passage is that the gifts of the Spirit have been given by God to His people until Jesus comes again, and until then we are to be guided by His love in how and when we use them.

The partial

Paul calls the gifts of the Spirit "the partial," and we need to understand why. Are they "partial" because they are imperfect? In other words, is he saying they are part right and part wrong; part God and part human in origin? Or does he call them "partial" because they are incomplete, limited, falling short of the full revelation of a matter? I think he answers this question in his letter to the Romans. There, in a chapter which emphasizes that believers are indwelt by the Holy Spirit, he says:

> "For we know that the whole creation groans and suffers the pains of childbirth together until now. And not only this, but also we ourselves, having the first fruits of the Spirit, even we ourselves groan within ourselves, waiting eagerly for [our] adoption as sons, the redemption of our body" (Ro 8:22-23).

Here he says believers are people who have "the first fruits of the Spirit," and he is using that term to refer to the baptism with the Holy Spirit and the gifts that accompany it. By calling that infusion of the Spirit a "first fruits," he's comparing it to a very familiar event in Judaism. The "first fruits" were a regular part of ancient Israel's worship (Lev 23:9-14; Dt 8:8). They were the first cutting or picking of a new harvest, and they were brought in to the temple and offered to God to honor Him as the Source of the entire harvest. They were only a small portion of the complete harvest that would soon follow. And of course, they must not be flawed or damaged in any way. They were cut from the very best section of the field, orchard or vineyard. So it was beautiful grain or fruit, yet it was incomplete; it was partial; it wasn't the whole field or orchard. So when Paul says, "For we know in part and we prophesy in part, but when the perfect comes the partial will be done away" (1Co 13:9-10), he's telling us that the gifts of the Spirit represent only a small portion of the full measure of blessings God has in store for us. When Jesus arrives and brings God's kingdom to earth, we will all have far more power and revelation than any gift of the Spirit could possibly give us now. Who will need a gift of healing after they're resurrected? Who will need a prophecy when all the promises have arrived? Who will need to speak in tongues when our old, fleshly mind is gone, and we can boldly approach the throne of God? And who will need a word of knowledge when we know as we are known?

Conclusion

So in one sense, we are all "cessationists" because we all recognize that Paul says the gifts of the Spirit will cease. The question we must answer is not "Will they cease?" but "When did Paul say they would cease?" And your answer and mine to that question will depend on what or who we believe "the perfect" is. Is it the completion of the New Testament, or is it the arrival of Jesus Christ? And our answer will dramatically affect the way we live out our discipleship. It will determine whether we view the book of Acts as a model that we are to follow or merely a history that we are to admire. It will either press us to seek to do what Jesus did or caution us to reject the supernatural because "those things are not for today." In this chapter I've given you my answer. What's yours?

Chapter Nine

The New You

Ezekiel 36:25-27

God's plan is for a profound transformation to take place inside those who believe in His Son, and a central element in that transformation is the baptism with the Holy Spirit.

So far in our study of the Holy Spirit, we have recognized that He is a distinct Person of God along with the Father and Son, and that it is through Him that much of God's work is performed. We have recognized that we humans were designed by God to live in the presence of the Holy Spirit, and that without His help we are doomed to fail in every important area of life. We have recognized that sin not only separates our spirit from God, but contaminates our physical bodies, so until Jesus' death and resurrection provided a sacrifice that was able to cleanse the sin contained in those bodies, the Holy Spirit could not dwell inside us. We marveled at the fact that the Son of God took on our sinful flesh and died on the cross so our bodies could become a tabernacle of God. We have recognized that John the Baptist was a prophet uniquely prepared by God to introduce Jesus to the world, and that he declared four essential truths about Him: First, He is the Lamb of God who takes away our sins; second, He is the pre-existent One who came to us from eternity; third, He is the Baptizer with the Holy Spirit; and fourth, He is the divine, begotten Son of God. We have recognized that the great outpouring of the Holy Spirit, promised by the prophets of Israel, began to arrive on the day of Pentecost and is still available to every person who repents and believes in Jesus Christ. We have recognized that the Holy Spirit is given "without measure" to every believer, but that there must be a human response to that gift which welcomes Him to dwell inside us and is willing to step out in faith so that His power and gifts can be released. And we have recognized that the Holy Spirit wants us to surrender our tongue so He can release our spirit to pray and praise in a language we don't understand. So now with these truths in mind, let's look more closely at the changes that take place inside us when we trust Jesus as our Savior and welcome the baptism with the Holy Spirit. And then let's consider how these changes will inevitably alter our future. For everyone who has experienced these changes, in this chapter we will be describing the "new you."

A new heart

When properly proclaimed, and when sincerely believed, the gospel produces a deep, internal miracle; it changes the basic orientation of the human heart. The prophet Ezekiel describes it this way:

> "Then I will sprinkle clean water on you, and you will be clean; I will cleanse you from all your filthiness and from all your idols. Moreover, I will give you a new heart and put a new spirit within you; and I will remove the heart of stone from your flesh and give you a heart of flesh" (Eze 36:25-26).

Every teaching in the New Testament is designed to lead a person to these changes or speaks to people in whom it is assumed that these changes have already taken place. The Bible does not try to teach untransformed people how to become better people. It doesn't push those who are still rebellious, selfish and independent to try harder to be good. It doesn't tell those who have not yet received a new heart that every time they sin, God's grace covers them. Unlimited grace is promised only to those who have had their "heart of stone" pulled out and a "heart of flesh" put in its place, to those who have come to love God and who long to please Him, in other words, to those who have become the "children of God." To announce such grace to the untransformed, to the still-rebellious, only encourages them to continue sinning. It calms any worry that God might hold them accountable for their actions. But to those true children of God who long to obey the Father but have failed to find victory over an area of temptation, the message of unlimited grace assures them that God will be patient while they learn to put "to death the deeds of the body" by the Spirit (Ro 8:13).

According to Ezekiel the first thing God will do is "cleanse" us from our sins. We understand that to mean that when we repent and believe in Jesus Christ, our sins are completely washed away so that there is no record of them before God. And we've already discussed the second thing God will do. Ezekiel says He will take out the rebellious spirit we inherited from Adam and Eve and put in its place an obedient heart. That means that everyone who is "born from above" (Jn 3:3) will desire to please God. He or she will not want to keep on sinning but will sincerely try to stop. And it is to those who have this transformed heart that Ezekiel says God will give a third gift. Listen:

> "I will put My Spirit within you and cause you to walk in My statutes, and you will be careful to observe My ordinances" (Eze 36:27).

Those words describe the baptism with the Holy Spirit which would be given when the Messiah brought God's kingdom to earth. In fact, this must be one of the verses to which Jesus was referring when He spoke to His disciples about "the promise of the Father" (Lk 24:49; Ac 1:4). When that day arrived, God would enable His people to fully walk according to His "statutes" (His covenant requirements) and observe His "ordinances" (worship Him as He has asked to be worshiped). He would do this by placing His Holy Spirit within them, thereby enabling them to obey Him fully and to worship Him as He desires to be worshiped. Then they would live in the many blessings that He had planned for them (Eze 36:28-38).

A new power

In the book of Romans Paul explains that even when a person possesses a new heart and desires to please God, he or she still will not be able to obey Him without the Holy Spirit's help because the power of temptation is too strong. He says the person who doesn't have the Spirit's power, or doesn't know how to draw on the help His indwelling presence provides, will inevitably be overwhelmed by their bodily impulses because those impulses are simply too great to resist. They will end up saying something like this:

> "Wretched man that I am! Who will set me free from this body that is full of death?" (Ro 7:24, paraphrase).

But Paul doesn't leave a struggling believer trapped in that cycle of frustration. First, he reminds those who are "in Christ Jesus" that we are not under condemnation even when the power of our flesh overwhelms us (Ro 8:1). And second, he points to the indwelling presence of the Holy Spirit and reminds us of how powerful He is and says that if we learn to draw on His power, we can escape the control of our rebellious flesh. He describes the Holy Spirit as "the Spirit of Him who raised Jesus from the dead…" (Ro 8:11). He wants us to see that this One who lives inside us is far more powerful than the sinful appetites and attitudes that originate in our dying bodies. Once we learn how to let Him strengthen us, we will find that we are able to put to death the deeds of the flesh and obey God. And that knowledge will profoundly affect our future.

The new you

So the new you is a person whose past is forgiven and who now lives in continuous grace. The new you is a person who possesses a new heart that loves God and wants to obey Him. And the new you is a person whose very body has been indwelt by a power far greater than the power of any temptation that may come your way so that you are able to obey God and worship Him as He desires to be worshiped. In other words, the new you has been set free, not to go back to old things, but to hear God call you into His service, to discover the way He has made you and the gifts that He has placed within you, and to develop godly character so that you can walk in holiness and not have your destiny stolen by falling into the traps the devil places in your path. The new you makes vastly different choices than the old you, and as a result the course of your life is dramatically changed. You're learning the art of obedience. You're living with a sense of purpose. You're daily feeling His pleasure and recognizing His care in everything you do. And whenever you sin, the new you quickly confesses and repents so you continue to become the person God designed you to be in your mother's womb, which changes your fundamental attitude toward life itself: You're now grateful to be alive because each day provides you with another opportunity to partner with God in building His eternal family.

Confessing the new

God's plan for every one of His children is that we live victorious, fruitful lives, but many do not. When they sin, they feel condemned. When they try to stop, they discover they can't, and that pattern of continual failure leads them to despair. That's why the three truths Ezekiel taught us are so important. They are not religious clichés. They are not empty words. They are profound, spiritual realities. And the person who understands and walks in these realities will find the abundant life that Jesus promised, not an easy life, not a luxurious life, but a life that has a true goal. And each person now has the power to reach that goal.

When people talk about the baptism with the Holy Spirit, they usually focus on speaking in tongues and on the fact that the Holy Spirit enables us to be witnesses for Jesus Christ. And it does release wonderful gifts for ministry. But frequently overlooked is the fact that the baptism with the Holy Spirit also provides us with the power to obey God and live holy lives. We don't realize that once we learn to pray as we ought to pray and worship as we ought to worship, we become strengthened to the point that we can successfully put to death the deeds of the flesh, make good choices, walk in faith, and endure in our assignment for a long time.

Today, let's recognize the new things God has placed in our lives. Let's confess these three foundational truths that we have learned:

> First: I am forgiven. My spirit is no longer separated from God by a barrier of sin. He is my loving Father, and because I have been joined to Jesus, I have been given every good gift.
>
> Second: I have a new heart. I now truly love God and want to please Him. My old rebellion has been replaced by trust. My selfishness has been replaced by a longing to help others find the God who loves them. And my independence has been replaced by a hunger for the joy I feel when I am in His presence.
>
> Third: My body is no longer unclean. It has become a dwelling place for the Holy Spirit, and He has awakened my human spirit so that I can hear, see and feel the spiritual realities that I never understood before. I have learned that by the Spirit I can pray and praise until I become strong, and then I can do whatever He has asked me to do.

To the person who has genuinely repented and believed in Jesus Christ, to the person who has welcomed the baptism with the Holy Spirit, each of these statements is absolutely true, and if we choose to believe what God has said and live by those truths, we will find a new source of power so strong that it will change the course of our lives and guide us into the blessings God has planned for us. We will become:

> "...like a tree planted by the rivers of water that brings forth its fruit in its season; our leaf also shall not wither, and whatsoever we do shall prosper" (Ps 1:3, paraphrase).

Chapter Ten

Walking in the Spirit

Those who have been baptized with the Holy Spirit need to learn a very important skill. They need to learn how to be refreshed by the presence of the Holy Spirit over and over again. Here are some helpful insights about how to do this.

By sending the Holy Spirit Jesus made it possible for every believer to "walk in the Spirit." That means that it is now possible for each one of us to be led by God daily, and even situation by situation, and to be empowered to do the things He leads us to do. Paul summarized our new potential this way:

> "for God is the One who is working in you both to will [desire] and to work [to have the power to accomplish] for His good pleasure [those things which please Him]" (Php 2:13, literal).

Paul explains that the Holy Spirit will not only show us what God desires; He will teach us to desire the same things. And then along with that desire, He will give us the supernatural strength, wisdom and spiritual gifts to accomplish what He placed in our heart, whether that be the transformation of our character or great acts of service.

Jesus made this new "walk" possible, but not inevitable. Every believer is given the freedom to choose. God doesn't take away our will and force us to do the right thing. When we become children of God, our Heavenly Father trains us as an earthly father trains his children, so it's very important to Him that we learn to exercise our will wisely. He wants to teach us to think as He thinks, to love as He loves, to understand why certain things are evil and other things are good. He wants to guide our development until we genuinely desire what is right, not just do what is right. Actually, it is only after a person undergoes God's inner transformation that he or she becomes truly free to obey or disobey God. Before that, like all human beings, we are held in bondage to a rebellious, human spirit that we inherited from Adam and Eve and are overwhelmed by the impulses of our flesh.

A believer's battle (Gal 5:16-25)

Paul's letter to the churches in Galatia appears to be the first letter he wrote; at least it's the earliest one that has been preserved in the New Testament. It was written after his first missionary journey in A.D. 49. Why that is significant to this study is this: What Paul taught the Galatians in A.D. 49 is what he was still teaching the churches in Rome eight or nine years later (A.D. 57-58). This was a foundational truth he continued to teach throughout his ministry. In chapter five of Galatians in a condensed form, he describes the same battle between the flesh and the Spirit that he describes in more detail in chapters seven and eight of Romans. In both letters he pictures a believer who is helplessly trapped between two powerful forces, the flesh and the Spirit, and is frustrated because he or she wants to do the right thing but is unable to do it. And the solution Paul proposes in both letters is the same as well: In order to do what their new heart wants to do, that person must be led and empowered by the Holy Spirit. Let's listen to what he said to the Galatians and then to what he said to the Romans. We'll start with his description of the problem and then hear the solution:

> "For the flesh sets its desire against the Spirit, and the Spirit against the flesh; for these are in opposition [put in position to fight against, to withstand as an adversary] to one another, so that you may not do the things that you please" (Gal 5:17).

> "I find then the principle that evil is present in me, the one who wants to do good. For I joyfully concur with the law of God in the inner man, but I see a different law in the members of my body, waging war against the law of my mind and making me

> a prisoner of the law of sin which is in my members. Wretched man that I am! Who will set me free from the body of this death?" (Ro 7:21-24).

The solution Paul proposes to both the Galatians and the Romans is also the same. Listen:

> "But I say, walk by the Spirit, and you will not carry out the desires of the flesh" (Gal 5:16).
>
> "For what the Law [of Moses] could not do, weak as it was through the flesh, God [did]: sending His own Son in the likeness of sinful flesh and [as an offering] for sin, He condemned sin in the flesh, so that the requirement of the Law might be fulfilled in us, who do not walk according to [following after its lead, under its control] the flesh but according to the Spirit" (Ro 8:3-4).

And in both letters he emphasizes the importance of being "led by the Spirit":

> "But if you are led by the Spirit, you are not under the Law" (Gal 5:18).
>
> "For all who are led by the Spirit of God, these are the sons of God" (Ro 8:14).

Understanding the realities that Paul is describing in these passages is absolutely foundational if you and I are going to live the victorious life God intends for us. We must know that our flesh is not yet redeemed (Ro 8:23) and is still trying to influence us. We must know that the Holy Spirit, with all His gifts and power, has come to live inside us. And we must know that our human spirit has a choice it must make, time and again, about which influence it will follow.

The choice

Every believer can choose to listen to the thoughts being generated by our physical bodies (and the enemy) or to the thoughts being generated by the Holy Spirit. Paul describes the process this way:

> "For the ones [following] after the flesh set their minds on the things of the flesh, but the ones [following] after the Spirit, the things of the Spirit. For the mind of the flesh [is] death, but the mind of the Spirit [is] life and peace" (Ro 8:5-6, literal).

And you would think that it would be simple to choose between the two, and it would be except for this fact: the voice of the flesh is persistent and must be resisted, but the voice of the Spirit is gentle and must be deliberately pursued. Even if we don't yield to the flesh, its voice keeps tempting us in one way or another, and if we do yield, its voice grows much louder, immediately. It seems to constantly lurk beneath the surface of our thoughts waiting for us to become tired, lonely, hungry, angry or afraid. Yet generally, a person must choose to resist the flesh, take the steps necessary to awaken their consciousness of the Holy Spirit and then press through whatever barriers the flesh may place in their way in order to hear His voice and receive His strength. The Lord is free to speak to His people whenever He chooses, and thankfully He will, at times, communicate with us when we have done nothing to seek Him. But normally believers must build disciplines into their lives if they are to regularly walk in the Spirit. They must find ways on a daily, and even moment by moment, basis to silence the flesh and press into the Spirit. And the person who does this produces the "fruit of the Spirit": love, joy, peace, patience, kindness, goodness, faithfulness, gentleness and self-control (Gal 5:22). The person who refuses, and thereby reverts to being led by their flesh, is the person who will consistently fall back into "the deeds of the flesh": immorality, impurity, sensuality, idolatry, sorcery, enmities, strife, jealousy, outbursts of anger, disputes, dissensions, factions, envying, drunkenness, carousing, etc. (Gal 5:19-21).

So "walking in the Spirit" requires these four elements: First, a humble self-awareness that my flesh is still present and must be consistently resisted if I am to avoid the "deeds of the flesh"; second, the decision to daily, and situation by situation, "crucify" the flesh with its passions and desires (Gal 5:24); third, the confidence that the Holy Spirit dwells in me so I can access His guidance and strength any time I need Him; and fourth, the wisdom to build disciplines into my life which regularly restore my awareness of His presence and enable me to hear His voice.

Timeless disciplines

Simply put, "walking in the Spirit" is regularly and deliberately choosing to become conscious of the Holy Spirit's presence and then allowing His presence to refresh us and then, in that transformed condition, listening for His voice. And the methods for drawing into His presence are not new; in fact, they are timeless. But what is new is that the Spirit Himself helps those who have been baptized with the Holy Spirit to do them.

- He helps us worship the Father and the Son (Ac 2:11; 1Co 14:15-18; Eph 5:18-19; Col 3:16-17).
- He helps us pray (Ro 8:26-27; 1Co 14:14-15; Eph 6:18; Jude 1:20).
- He helps us understand the Word (Jn 14:16, 17, 26; 15:26; 1Co 2:12; 1Th 4:9; 1Jn 2:20-21, 27).

These three disciplines, worship, prayer and meditating on Scripture, have always been the means by which the men and women of God have drawn close to Him. And the baptism with the Holy Spirit doesn't replace these disciplines; it empowers us to do them at a new level. Now we can worship assisted by the Spirit and in the midst of that worship receive spiritual gifts which inspire, heal or guide us (1Co 12:7-11). We can pray at a new level with a new accuracy. When our own words fail us, we can let Him guide our tongue to ask for the things God wants us to ask for (Ro 8:27). And when we open the Bible, we are not left to our own speculations to discover its meaning. The Spirit becomes our Teacher and will explain its truths to us and speak to us from its pages as clearly as if we were having a conversation with someone in the room.

A personal reflection

It occurs to me that it might be helpful if I shared some of the disciplines that have become a regular part of my own life. I don't consider these to be the only way, or even the best way, but for me they have been proven by the test of time. I've done them for decades because they work. I do them, not because I ought to, but because I need to. Yet having said that, I'm sure there are new levels of relationship that the Lord will teach me in the future, and I will follow Him there as I can. For now my life includes:

A daily time of drawing near to the Lord in the morning. My goal is not to put in a certain amount of time, but to stay there until I become conscious of His presence.

I normally start by reading the Bible, and continue reading and mediating until "my heart gets happy" (George Mueller). Then I write down what I hear the Lord say to me through His Word.

Next, I follow the counsel of Philippians 4:6, to "Be anxious for nothing, but in everything by prayer and supplication with thanksgiving let your requests be made known to God." I unload my worries and wounds on Him through prayer until "the peace of God which passes all comprehension" guards my heart and mind. Some days have more than others. By the way, I do mention long lists of people in prayer, but I do that on another occasion during the day.

I nearly always pray in tongues for a while, and I also pray through the Lord's Prayer, item by item, making sure that I keep my thoughts focused on the Father and reflect on the meaning of each statement.

I confess my sins throughout the day as soon as I realize I have done them, and often take the bread and cup of communion to remind myself of the power of the cross. And whenever I take the bread and cup, I give to Jesus my sickness and sorrow as well as my sins.

It would be a mistake not to mention fasting. It helps me break the grip of the flesh when it becomes strong. I don't fast more than a meal or two at a time and always combine it with prayer and meditation. For some reason even this very minimal form of fasting breaks down spiritual barriers and empowers me to pray with fresh faith.

And finally, I should mention how important it is for me to worship with the gathered church. I seem to be able to press into the Spirit more easily when I am in the midst of my

> spiritual family. At some point during worship my emotions usually change, and my negative thoughts turn to hope. When that happens, I find fresh strength to face the future.

May the Lord guide each of us so that we learn how to "walk in the Spirit" and not "carry out the desire of the flesh" (Gal 5:16).

Chapter Eleven

His Seal and Pledge

Ephesians 1:13-14

The baptism with the Holy Spirit brings us many wonderful gifts, but one of the most precious gifts of all is the assurance of our salvation. Paul says the Holy Spirit testifies to our human spirit that we have been adopted by God as His children. And that assurance will protect us against the doubts that try to erode our confidence.

I've heard the gospel and accepted God's offer of salvation, but how do I know He accepts me? I prayed the sinner's prayer and meant every word I said, but is there a way God can prove to me that I am really saved? I know the Bible says that we are saved by faith, and I believe God's promise, but there are times when I've questioned my own faith. I have been so disappointed with myself that it made me wonder if I ever really believed. Is it possible for a person like me to be sure that they belong to God, to know without a doubt that they will step into heaven when they die? Or must some of us finish out our days desperately hoping we repented sincerely enough and believed wholeheartedly enough to receive eternal life?

Thankfully, the answer to that painful question is: Yes, we can know for sure that we are saved and will go to heaven when we die! The most important reason of all is the witness of Scripture. Over and over again, in many different ways, God states in His Word this truth: that the just shall live by faith (Hab 2:4). And if that were the only witness we had, it would be enough. But there is also another way God confirms to His children that we belong to Him, and Paul points to that way in his letter to the church in Ephesus. While reflecting on the founding of the church in that city (see Ac 18:18-21; 19:1-7), he describes in Ephesians 1:13-14 the process of how those Gentile men and women became part of God's great family, and in doing so lists three basic steps. First, he says they heard "the message of truth, the gospel of your salvation" (vs.13). Then, he says they believed what they heard. And finally, he says God sealed them with "the promised Holy Spirit" (vs. 13, literal) which he describes as "a pledge of our inheritance" which will last until God's "purchased treasure is redeemed" (v14, literal). And it is in this third step that Paul reveals the other voice that will calm our fears, the witness who, along with Scripture, will confirm that we are children of God. When we understand what Paul means when he says that the Holy Spirit is our "seal" and "pledge," the doubts about our salvation need never trouble us again.

Seal and pledge

In ancient cultures seals were a common part of life. The person who carried a seal carried with them the authority of the one who sent them. The contents of a container might be sealed to ensure that nothing had been removed or changed. Seals were a mark indicating approval and authenticity, which explains why Jesus used the image of the seal when speaking of the Father's approval of Him. Referring to Himself as the Son of Man, He said, "... for on Him the Father, God, has set His seal" (Jn 6:27). He was making staggering claims about Himself, but He didn't ask people to believe those claims without proof. And as we read through the gospels, we can recognize numerous ways God set His "seal" on Jesus thereby proving His claims: a voice from heaven (Mt 3:17); the impartation of the Holy Spirit (Mt 3:16); John the Baptist's testimony (Jn 1:6-8, 15, 29-34; 3:26-36; 5:33-36); the many miracles Jesus performed; and the specific prophecies He fulfilled (Jn 5:38-39). Of course, the greatest confirmation of all was Jesus' resurrection from the dead (Jn 2:19-22; 20:1-9).

The Greek word Paul uses in Ephesians 1:14, which we often translate as "pledge," is arrabon. It can also be translated as "earnest money" or "down payment." In modern Greek the word arrabona means an engagement ring (W.E. Vine, An Expository Dictionary of New Testament Words, Fleming Revell, 1966, Vol.2, p.11). In Paul's day it was used in business transactions to refer to the earnest money paid by a buyer to a seller. That money was forfeited if the purchase was not completed, so the amount needed to be large enough to prove that the buyer was sincerely committed to pay the rest of what was owed. By calling the Holy Spirit a "pledge [arrabon] of our inheritance," Paul is saying that God has given the Holy Spirit to us with such evident power that this gift is like a down payment. Our experience with the Spirit now is so real, so tangible and so observable that it proves God will give us the full measure of our inheritance when Jesus returns to set up God's kingdom on earth.

Application

Now let's apply this truth to our own lives. Let's answer the question: How does the Holy Spirit serve as a "seal of our salvation" and a "pledge of our inheritance?" In other words, how do the baptism with the Holy Spirit and the gifts that are released when we receive His infilling prove to us and to others that we belong to God? And how does it change the way we view our future? Here are four ways:

First, the Spirit's presence within us is an assurance to our hearts that we are saved. Paul tells us that the Holy Spirit testifies to our human spirit that we are children of God. Listen:

> "For you have not received a spirit of slavery leading to fear again, but you have received a spirit of adoption as sons by which we cry out, 'Abba! Father!' The Spirit Himself witnesses with our spirit that we are children of God, and if children, also heirs, heirs of God and fellow heirs of Christ…" (Ro 8:15-17, literal).
>
> "Because you are sons, God has sent forth the Spirit of His Son into our hearts, crying, 'Abba! Father!' Therefore you are no longer a slave, but a son; and if a son, then an heir through God" (Gal 4:6-7).

Paul is telling us that one of the greatest comforts the Comforter brings is His inner voice telling us that we are saved. When we encounter God through the power of the Holy Spirit, the way we think about God changes. He becomes more than a concept; He becomes Someone we know personally.

His touch assures us that we are clean. His presence assures us that we are not alone. His voice assures us that we are His children. And it is this assurance that produces dignity and boldness.

Second, the Spirit's presence at work in and through us is also confirmation to other believers that God has accepted us. It allows them to trust us and include us in their gatherings. We see this happening in the book of Acts when Jewish believers in Jerusalem heard that Gentiles in Samaria had been water-baptized and thereby welcomed into the church. They were doubtful that Gentiles who had not yet become Jews could be saved, and they were shocked that ceremonially unclean people had been brought into the fellowship of the church, until they heard that those Gentiles were baptized with the Holy Spirit. Listen:

> "'And as I [Peter] began to speak, the Holy Spirit fell upon them just as He [did] upon us at the beginning ["speaking with tongues and exalting God," Ac 10:46]. And I remembered the word of the Lord, how He used to say, "John baptized with water, but you will be baptized with the Holy Spirit." Therefore if God gave to them the same gift as [He gave] to us also after believing in the Lord Jesus Christ, who was I that I could stand in God's way?' When they heard this, they quieted down and glorified God, saying, 'Well then, God has granted to the Gentiles also the repentance [that leads] to life'" (Ac 11:15-18).

> "After there had been much debate, Peter stood up and said to them [the Jerusalem Council], 'Brethren, you know that in the early days God made a choice among you, that by my mouth the Gentiles would hear the word of the gospel and believe. And God, who knows the heart, testified to them giving them the Holy Spirit, just as He also did to us; and He made no distinction between us and them, cleansing their hearts by faith'" (Ac 15:7-9).

Based on the fact that God had baptized a group of people with the Holy Spirit, with the visible evidence of speaking in tongues and prophetic praise, the leaders of the early church put aside their fears and accepted them even though they were culturally very different from themselves.

Third, the Spirit's presence in us and His powerful works through us are proof to the watching world that Jesus is the Savior. Words alone are not enough. People need to see the God we proclaim change lives and do wonders. The early church needed God's power to prove to Israel that Jesus was the promised Messiah and to the Greek world that the resurrection actually happened. And in the atmosphere in which we minister today, that same power is still needed to prove to skeptics that God exists. Those who watch us need to see that if they receive Jesus as their Savior, He will help them in their suffering. They need to see that the power of the Spirit can break addictions, release depression, provide comfort for the lonely and guide the confused. The gifts of the Spirit, when functioning properly, may be needed more now than they have ever been. The Bible is full of examples of the Spirit's presence serving as proof to a watching world; here are two:

> "But Peter and the apostles answered… 'The God of our fathers raised up Jesus, whom you had put to death by hanging Him on a cross. He is the one whom God exalted to His right hand as a Prince and Savior, to grant repentance to Israel, and forgiveness of sins. And we are witnesses of these things; and so [is] the Holy Spirit, whom God has given to those who obey Him'" (Ac 5:29-32).

> "And it happened that the father of Publius was lying [in bed] afflicted with [recurrent] fever and dysentery; and Paul went in [to see] him and after he had prayed, he laid his hands on him and healed him. After this had happened, the rest of the people on the island [Malta] who had diseases were coming to him and getting cured" (Ac 28:8-9).

And fourth, the Holy Spirit is not only a <u>seal</u> to us; Paul says He is also a <u>pledge</u>, and as such His presence reminds us of the glorious inheritance waiting for us at the end of this age. We know our eternal future will be one in which we will be immersed in the unrestrained glory of God to such a degree of intensity that we need a resurrected body to endure it. But the thought of being immersed in God's unrestrained glory isn't strange or frightening to us; it's thrilling because in this life we have already experienced beautiful moments of being immersed in His love. So the thought of an eternity in which there will be more of that is… heavenly. And we are absolutely certain of that future because we have received God's pledge: The same Spirit who raised Jesus from the dead now dwells in us (Ro 8:11). We have the "first fruits of the Spirit" (Ro 8:23). We've tasted "... the powers of the age to come" (Heb 6:5). So it's no wonder Paul prayed the following prayer for believers in Ephesus and for us:

> "I [pray that] the eyes of your heart may be enlightened, so that you will know what is the hope of His calling, what are the riches of the glory of His inheritance in the saints, and what is the surpassing greatness of His power toward us who believe..." (Eph 1:18-19).

Conclusion

What we've learned today is that after someone <u>hears</u> the gospel and <u>believes</u> it, they also need to be <u>sealed</u> with the Holy Spirit. That means they need to be baptized with the Holy Spirit and have the gifts of the Spirit at work in their lives. We've learned that this is God's plan for all of us; it's one of the great gifts He gives to His children. It's His "sealing" that assures us that we are saved, that confirms to others that we have been accepted by God, that proves to a watching world that Jesus is indeed the One who can save them and that continually reminds us that the rest of our inheritance will surely be given to us in the age to come. To leave someone without the confidence this "seal" and "pledge" is designed to give them is to leave them vulnerable to doubts and fears; it is to leave them without an important resource that God intended for them to have. And once we understand this truth, each of us needs to ask ourselves, "Do I have this resource?" And each of us needs to commit to helping others receive it.

Section Two

The Spirit and the Gathered Church

This section takes the reader passage by passage through chapters 12, 13 and 14 of First Corinthians. We focus on this portion of this great letter because nowhere else in the Bible is there a detailed description of how the gifts of the Spirit are supposed to function when the church gathers. Though Paul wrote these chapters to correct wrong behavior, in them we hear him coach people in how to properly minister in the Spirit. And what he taught them still applies today, so we can use these teachings to guide our gatherings as well.

Now concerning spiritual gifts, brethren,
I do not want you to be unaware.

1Corinthians 12:1

Chapter Twelve

Testing Prophecy

[1]Now concerning spiritual gifts, brethren, I do not want you to be unaware. [2]You know that when you were pagans, you were led astray to the mute idols, however you were led. [3]Therefore I make known to you that no one speaking by the Spirit of God says, "Jesus is accursed"; and no one can say, "Jesus is Lord," except by the Holy Spirit.

1 Corinthians 12:1-3

The baptism with the Holy Spirit is a gift God gives to an individual. The Spirit of God comes to dwell within the "temple" of that person's body. And as we've seen in previous chapters, this indwelling is essential equipment if we are going to fulfill Jesus' expectation that His earthly ministry would be continued through us. For that to happen we must be able to speak what we hear Him say and do what we see Him do, just as He followed the Father's lead in everything He did and said (Jn 5:19; 8:28). Our spiritual senses must be awakened, and we must learn to allow the Holy Spirit to minister through us. And then there is one more essential step that we must take. The Lord's plan for His church was never based on a model in which His followers would operate independently of one another. He expected every one of us to become part of a community of believers. He would be our Head, and we, as various members of His corporate "body," would work together as a team to carry His salvation to our Jerusalem, Judea, Samaria and the remotest parts of the earth. But when we read church history, we discover that the church only functioned as a Spirit-led community for a few centuries. Its family-like gatherings were soon replaced by hierarchical structures and liturgical services, which are not wrong in themselves, but certainly differ from the gatherings of the early church.

The clearest picture of how the gifts of the Spirit operated in the gatherings of the early church is found in chapters twelve, thirteen and fourteen of First Corinthians. In those chapters we hear Paul correcting certain attitudes and errors in the way the Corinthian believers were conducting themselves. And if we listen closely, we can picture in our minds what was taking place. We see believers meeting in homes with individuals contributing to the upbuilding of the whole assembly by expressing various spiritual gifts. And Paul lists the most common forms of those gifts (1Co 12:8-10) and then gives strong pastoral instruction on how and when they should be used. Because these chapters are unique in their description of a church service during the apostolic period, in this section entitled "The Spirit and the Gathered Church," we will examine them passage by passage in order to learn from Paul how the Holy Spirit desires to minister through us today.

A troubled church

Paul was the apostle who introduced the gospel to the city of Corinth, and he pastored the church there for the first year and a half of its existence (Ac 18:1-11). About five years after he left the city, he wrote a letter to them that we call First Corinthians, and as we read through this letter, we soon recognize that the church faced many serious challenges after he left (Ac 20:29-30). Here is a list of some of the problems he tried to correct: the congregation had divided itself into groups that were loyal to different leaders based in part on who had baptized them (1:11-13); Greek philosophy and mental pride was eroding basic truths of the gospel among some (2:14); certain rich, powerful individuals were openly criticizing Paul because of the suffering and poverty he endured as an apostle (4:8); a blatant case of incest was being ignored (5:1), visits to temple prostitutes by church members were being tolerated (6:15); church members were suing each other in secular courts (6:6); married couples were practicing celibacy (7:1-5) and divorcing (7:10-13); Gentile believers were living like Jews, and Jewish believers were living like Gentiles (7:17-20); the whole church was facing a "present distress" (7:26) so severe that Paul thought it might be the beginning of events leading up to the return of Christ (7:26-31; 2Th 1-2); some members of the church were asserting their freedom in Christ to do things that troubled the conscience of weaker believers, and by their example had pressured some into doing things they believed were wrong (8:9-13); certain voices were claiming that Paul wasn't a valid apostle because he didn't fit their unbiblical criteria; he didn't travel with a wife or receive financial offerings (9:1-15); some of the women in the church, recognizing their spiritual freedom in Christ, were uncovering their heads during worship gatherings which was an immodest action in that culture (11:5-6); when fellowship meals were held, some people refused to share the food they brought with others, and poorer members were left hungry (11:20-22, 33-34); some even got drunk on the wine they had brought to celebrate the Lord's Supper (11:21); and, finally, some were teaching a flagrant heresy that claimed believers will never be physically resurrected from the dead (15:12-19).

So as we study through chapters 12-14 of First Corinthians, it's helpful to keep in mind the serious problems that troubled this particular church because some of the underlying attitudes that caused those problems also affected the way they ministered in the gifts of the Holy Spirit. Let's face it: Corinth was <u>not</u> a healthy church. So as we read through these chapters, we often encounter situations where we must learn the right way to do things in a worship service by listening to Paul correct the wrong ways they did them. Yet we need to be very careful when we do that. It would be a mistake to assume that Paul's ultimate goal was to stop the Corinthians from ministering in the gifts of the Spirit. He was not finding fault with the gifts themselves, he was finding fault with the way they were being used. He was trying to stop wrong behaviors and replace them with right behaviors. He wanted these zealous believers to continue moving freely in the Spirit, but when they did so to be guided by the same selfless love that led Jesus to the cross. He was cautioning them to prioritize the needs of others, avoid pride and do nothing that would draw the attention of the congregation away from Jesus. His goal was to ensure that the gifts of the Spirit would not cease to be practiced because of misuse.

Concerning spiritual things (1Co 12:1-3)

Paul begins his explanation of the operations of the Holy Spirit (pneumatikos, literally: "spirituals") by reminding the Corinthians that not all spiritual manifestations are from God. The devil can also "inspire" prophecies and do wonders. Oracles, divinations and even healings were a familiar part of the Greek religions of that day, yet the guidance and power that people received from those sources didn't lead them toward the true God or salvation; it led them into deception and bondage to demons (1Co 10:19-21). So Paul begins this entire discussion by telling the Corinthian church that he doesn't want them to be ignorant, meaning untaught, naïve or gullible when it comes to the proper operation of the supernatural gifts of the Spirit. He reinforces his warning by reminding them of what happened to them in the past when they didn't know how to distinguish a true prophecy from a false one. And then he gives them a simple criterion to separate what's true from what's false. Here it is:

> "For this reason I make known to you that no one speaking in the Spirit of God says, 'anathema [literal: set apart for God's destruction], Jesus,' and no one can say, 'Lord Jesus' except in the Holy Spirit" (v3, literal).

Paul uses an example of extreme blasphemy against Jesus, but it was probably not that uncommon at the time. The gospel was a new message confronting established religions, and it often faced violent opposition, both physically and verbally from Judaism and Gentile cults. In the book of Acts Luke describes the gospel coming to Corinth and notes that some members of that synagogue had responded to Paul's preaching with blasphemy (Ac 18:5-6). And that blasphemy may well have included the words "anathema Jesus," and on occasion may have come in the form of "prophetic" denunciation of Him. It's even possible that this terrible phrase matches the very words Saul of Tarsus tried to extract from Christians as he whipped them in the synagogues (Ac 26:11). The word "anathema" is Greek, but it is the very word which is used in the Greek translation of the Bible when something or someone is set apart for destruction (Lev 27:28-29: Nu 21:3; Dt 7:26; 13:17; Mic 4:13). And Judaism wasn't alone in its opposition to the gospel. The oracles and diviners in the idol temples surely "prophesied" against Jesus as well. So Paul is speaking to people in Corinth who likely had heard all sorts of prophecies, some of which even pretended to be God condemning Jesus. And he is telling them to be cautious about accepting a spiritual manifestation just because someone says it's from God… even if that manifestation comes in a church service. The question he wanted them to ask themselves when they listened to something claiming to be prophetic is:

Does this word come from the Spirit of God, or is it from some other source? And if you and I don't learn to ask ourselves that same question, we too will be led astray. Each of us must learn to separate what's true from what's false.

The problem with prophecy

The most dangerous aspect of prophecy is that it is supposed to be God who is speaking, and if God says something, who can argue with it? After all, He's God! So our inclination when we hear a prophecy is to set our judgment aside and passively accept what we hear, even if it doesn't seem right. We assume God must know something we don't, and indeed there are times when God is telling us things we don't understand or find hard to believe, and in those situations the proper response is to humbly submit. But this is where prophecy becomes dangerous; just because someone claims to be speaking for God doesn't mean they are. We may be listening to something that is nothing more than that person's own thoughts on a matter expressed in prophetic language, or even worse, it could be something motivated by the enemy. And to make the situation even more complicated, sometimes part of what is said is from God, and part of it is merely that person's own thoughts. The result is a mixture of inspiration and flesh, leaving us to try to discern which is which. And we must also be able to discern such things not only in others but in ourselves as well. Are we aware when we stop speaking God's Word and start speaking our own? Are we humble enough to stop mid-sentence and confess to others when we make a mistake? Since the baptism with the Holy Spirit places the Giver of all gifts within each believer, every one of us is capable of prophesying when the Spirit leads us (1Co 14:31). What separates an effective prophecy from a mixed or false one is not the capacity to prophesy but the integrity with which we do it. In prophecy, as in everything else, human will and a person's integrity are involved. Do we speak only what we hear Him say and stop when He stops? Do we monitor our attitude and refuse to allow temper, pride or fear to affect what we say or the way we say it? It is our integrity, our knowledge of Scripture, our submission to the Lord and our love for His people which are the main factors that determine whether or not we are effective in ministering any of the spiritual gifts. A person who seeks to speak on God's behalf but lacks these qualities produces far more trouble than help. They mislead, confuse, condemn and cause others to "despise prophetic utterances" (1Th 5:20). Some may "prophesy" because they desire attention; some may use it to dominate a gathering; some may "prophesy" as a way of trying to force God to act; and some simply say the same things over and over again.

Test everything

But in spite of these dangers, when prophecy is genuine, it edifies, exhorts and comforts God's people (1Co 14:3). It enables us to hear God, and hearing His voice always brings life. So even though there may be problems like those mentioned above, the benefits that come from this gift are so great that we must learn to prophesy properly, not discard it. Paul models this approach in the way he counsels the church in Thessalonica. Apparently that congregation was experiencing false or loveless prophecy which is why Paul wrote these words:

> "Do not quench [put out a fire] the Spirit, do not despise [consider to be worthless] prophecies. But examine [approve after testing] everything carefully; hold fast [take hold of and keep] to that which is good; abstain [hate] from every form [outward expression] of evil" (1Th 5:19-22, paraphrase).

Do we hear what Paul is saying? He says in effect, "Don't let false prophecy cause you to stop longing for true prophecy." The greatest danger of the false is that it takes away our appetite for the genuine. It leaves us cynical. We "sit in the seat of the scornful" (Ps 1:1). We dismiss all prophecy and thus silence the Holy Spirit. But Paul says the answer is not to withdraw but to become more discerning, to stay so committed to hearing a true word from God that we won't tolerate a false word; to test, confront and even discipline if necessary. And as we do these things, we will always choose to be kind to each other, never mean. There must always be room for mistakes when people are learning.

Conclusion

If any person or any church is going to grow in the spiritual gifts (pneumatikos) they must accept the responsibility to grow stronger in their ability to recognize the voice of God. There will always be mistakes because we are human, so we must learn to separate the wheat from the chaff. Paul wrote to a Corinthian church that had much trouble in its use of the spiritual gifts, but he didn't tell them to stop expressing those gifts; he told them to grow in the way they were expressing them. So the question before you and me today is: will we grow? Scripture will always be our final authority in all matters of faith and practice. No prophetic word will ever be compared in value or authority to God's written Word. All that is spoken will always be tested by Scripture. Yet because God still desires to speak to His people to comfort, exhort and edify us, maybe even to warn us, how we answer that question will either silence Him or open our ears. Will you and I accept the responsibility to be discerning so He can continue to speak to us?

Chapter Thirteen

When We Gather

[4]Now there are varieties of gifts, but the same Spirit. [5]And there are varieties of ministries, and the same Lord. [6]There are varieties of effects, but the same God who works all things in all persons. [7]But to each one is given the manifestation of the Spirit for the common good. [8]For to one is given the word of wisdom through the Spirit, and to another the word of knowledge according to the same Spirit; [9]to another faith by the same Spirit, and to another gifts of healing by the one Spirit, [10]and to another the effecting of miracles, and to another prophecy, and to another the distinguishing of spirits, to another various kinds of tongues, and to another the interpretation of tongues. [11]But one and the same Spirit works all these things, distributing to each one individually just as He wills.

I Corinthians 12:4-11

The Holy Spirit was not only sent by Jesus to dwell within individual believers, He was also given to the church to dwell among us. When we gather together to worship and hear God's Word, the Holy Spirit is there with us as surely as our Lord Jesus promised to be with us (Mt 18:20). In these chapters of First Corinthians (12-14) Paul is not talking about individual believers or the universal church, which is made up of every believer everywhere. He's talking about what happens when groups of believers gather in homes or on a riverbank or under the shade of a large tree. There were no church buildings in those days. Those who loved Jesus came together as a local expression of the family of God. And something special happened when they did. Jesus assured us that it would when He said this: "For where two or three have gathered together in My name, I am there in their midst" (Mt 18:20). He's telling us that a group doesn't have to be large to be considered a church, but it does have to be more than one. You and I have been called by God, not only to Himself, but also to each other. He never intended for us to live out our spiritual lives alone.

If we were to describe the problems of the Corinthian church, we would probably place these two attitudes at the top of our list: pride and selfishness. They didn't think they needed each other, at least they didn't need those who were poor or different, and when they did get together, their focus was entirely on themselves. So it's amazing that even though he was writing to people with such wrong attitudes, Paul was still very patient in the way he dealt with them. Carefully, step by step, he explained how Jesus' church was supposed to function. He said every member should be involved. He emphasized the fact that God values and cares for each person, so no one should be overlooked or considered unnecessary. His goal was to change the way they thought about gathering together. He wanted them to treasure those gatherings and to see how important they were. And he wanted them to treasure each other as well, not merely looking past their various differences but seeing those differences as a beautiful part of God's plan.

Graces, ministries and changed hearts (vs4-6)

Paul begins by explaining how the Father, Son and Holy Spirit are all involved in the care of the church. Using a Greek word that describes something being divided into portions, and then those portions being deliberately given to certain people, he describes what the Holy Spirit does, what the Lord Jesus does and what the Father does. Starting with the Spirit, he says when the church gathers, the Holy Spirit distributes a "grace" to each person. The word in verse four that is so often translated as "gift" actually means "a grace" because it is a gift that is completely undeserved. In other words the Spirit chooses to distribute a particular blessing to someone, not because that person deserves to be helped, but because he or she is loved by God. Next, Paul tells us that Jesus, as the Head of His Church, distributes different ministries to different people. Under His guidance we all serve Him in different ways, but since He is the one who's leading us, the result is not chaos or individualism but a harmonious and coordinated community through which His full ministry is released. It's as though Jesus Himself walks among us and cares for us as freely as He cared for His disciples before He ascended into heaven. And finally, Paul tells us that our Heavenly Father is guiding this entire process toward a particular goal, and that goal is that each person's heart will be changed to become more and more like His Son (Ro 8:29). The One who searches our hearts (Ro 8:27) and knows exactly what each of us needs works powerfully inside us to transform our attitudes and develop our character.

Each one (v7)

Later on in this chapter (12:12-27) Paul will discuss the ministries that Jesus assigns to each of us, but at this verse he begins to describe how the Holy Spirit ministers to each of us when we gather:

> "And to each one is given the revelation of the Holy Spirit in order to assist that person to carry the load that they are bearing" (v7, paraphrase).

The way one particular Greek word in this verse is translated affects the meaning of the entire passage that follows. That word is "sumphero." Its literal meaning is "to carry with," but it has traditionally been translated as "the common good" or "to profit withal." At its basic level the word pictures someone coming up to someone else who is carrying a heavy load and saying, "Here, let me help you carry that." So the word may be better translated as "help" or "assistance," and if we accept that translation, then what Paul is saying is this: "When you gather as a church, the Holy Spirit has a grace for each one of you designed specifically to meet your need. He knows the weight that is on you, and He will help you carry it."

Paul wanted the Corinthians to understand how much God valued each person who came into their gatherings, and in light of that truth to do the same. So he carefully explained how the Holy Spirit distributes different gifts to different people based on His knowledge of their different needs. His purpose in doing this went far beyond providing that church with a comprehensive list of the gifts of the Holy Spirit. He wanted them to realize what was happening in the spiritual realm when they gathered for worship: The Spirit was coming among them to distribute His gifts to each one based on His complete knowledge of each person's needs. In some cases He might give His gift directly to that person, while in others He might give it through someone else. But regardless of how His "grace" was delivered, it was always an expression of His loving care, and there was always something available for each one. By revealing this remarkable insight Paul was teaching the Corinthian church (and us) that times of corporate worship are a dynamic opportunity for those who are present to be healed, counselled or strengthened by the Holy Spirit.

The "graces" of the Spirit (vs8-10)

Then Paul lists some of the common ways the Holy Spirit helps us. To the one who lacks wisdom, He will reveal the wisdom you need. You will suddenly see your situation from God's perspective. To the one who lacks knowledge, the Holy Spirit will supernaturally provide information. To the one who lacks the faith to receive salvation or lay hold of a particular promise, He will impart faith to your heart. Suddenly you will believe. To those who are ill, He will send His healing presence to cure different kinds of sickness. To the one who needs a miraculous work of God's power, His presence will empower you, free you or provide the help you need. To the one who needs to hear God speak to them, who needs to be edified, exhorted, comforted or even warned, God will send a prophecy either directly to you or through someone else in the gathering. To the one who is unable to identify the spiritual source at work in a particular situation, whether the source is God, the flesh or the devil, the Holy Spirit will reveal the truth to you. To the one who needs to praise and give thanks to God without their own thoughts interfering, the Spirit will enable you to do so in languages you've never learned. And if the Spirit desires that praise and thanksgiving to be heard by the rest of the church, He will prompt you to speak out in that unlearned language so all can hear, and will then provide a translation of what you said so that all can understand and be helped by it.

When we gather (v11)

Finally, Paul concludes his description of the many different ways the Holy Spirit ministers to us with this summary:

> "And all these things [all the "graces" described above] the one and the same Spirit works in all [of us], distributing [His gifts] to each one, individually, just as He wills" (v11, literal).

That's the truth Paul wanted the Corinthians to see: When God's people gather, the Holy Spirit comes among them and graciously reaches out to each person. He doesn't have favorites; it's all based on grace. He doesn't care for one and ignore another. He knows the need of each person and gives to each one just what they need. And Paul's point is this: If God sees His Church like that, if He treasures each one and cares for them so tenderly, shouldn't we? Shouldn't we see the gathering of God's people as a holy assembly in which the Spirit is powerfully at work? Shouldn't we stop withholding ourselves from those who are poor or broken or come from different backgrounds? Shouldn't we love each other like God loves us?

Conclusion

Earlier in this letter (1Co 11:17-34) Paul warned the Corinthians that they did not recognize the presence of Jesus in the Lord's Supper. They had divided themselves into hostile groups and had become disrespectful toward the bread and cup. Now in this chapter he's warning them that they didn't recognize God's presence among them when they gathered to worship either. Many came only to receive a blessing for themselves and felt no responsibility for the spiritual well-being of others. To counter that attitude Paul showed them what happens in the spiritual realm when God's people gather. The Spirit distributes "graces" to all; the Lord Jesus leads His people into the ministries to which He has called them, and the Father works powerfully within each heart to make us more like Jesus. Paul showed them all of this so that when they gathered, they would "judge the body rightly" (1Co 11:29). Do we?

Chapter Fourteen

The Body of Christ

[12]For even as the body is one and yet has many members, and all the members
of the body, though they are many, are one body, so also is Christ. [13]For
by one Spirit we were all baptized into one body, whether Jews or Greeks,
whether slaves or free, and we were all made to drink of one Spirit. [14]For
the body is not one member, but many. [15]If the foot says, "Because I am not
a hand, I am not a part of the body," it is not for this reason any the less a
part of the body. [16]And if the ear says, "Because I am not an eye, I am not a
part of the body," it is not for this reason any the less a part of the body. [17]If
the whole body were an eye, where would the hearing be? If the whole were
hearing, where would the sense of smell be? [18]But now God has placed the
members, each one of them, in the body, just as He desired. [19]If they were
all one member, where would the body be? [20]But now there are many
members, but one body. [21]And the eye cannot say to the hand, "I have no
need of you"; or again the head to the feet, "I have no need of you." [22]On
the contrary, it is much truer that the members of the body which seem to
be weaker are necessary; [23]and those members of the body which we deem
less honorable, on these we bestow more abundant honor, and our less
presentable members become much more presentable, [24]whereas our more
presentable members have no need of it. But God has so composed the
body, giving more abundant honor to that member which lacked, [25]so that
there may be no division in the body, but that the members may have the
same care for one another. [26]And if one member suffers, all the members
suffer with it; if one member is honored, all the members rejoice with it.
[27]Now you are Christ's body, and individually members of it.

1 Corinthians 12:12-27

We all come into the family of God with our thinking conditioned by a human culture that values certain kinds of people and devalues others. In this passage Paul is telling the church in Corinth that they must actively work against the pride and shame produced by those old ways of thinking. Those who came from a Jewish background must gladly welcome those who didn't. They must understand that in Christ every believer holds equal status and enjoys the same privileges. Those who came from wealth or a high social position must not separate themselves from those who are poor or come from difficult situations. And the reverse is also true. Those from humble backgrounds must not disqualify themselves because of their former religion or social status. They must not compare themselves to others and decide that they are not needed. Paul says the Lord wants all believers to think of themselves as members of a team in which every person's contribution is important, and to illustrate that he compares the Church to a human body in which every part is necessary and belongs to the whole.

But as Paul continues this teaching, we discover that the attitude that values certain kinds of people and devalues others doesn't stop at religious backgrounds or social position. If left unchecked, it will also look down on people who minister differently than we do. It forgets that Jesus calls people to a wide variety of ministries in His Church so that a diverse range of needs can be met. Paul tells the Corinthians that this diversity of ministry should be welcomed, not rejected. No one should reject the way God has designed him or her, nor envy others. The church that Jesus draws together will always be made up of many different kinds of people with many different kinds of ministries. And in His church there is to be no hierarchy of value. Every person, every ministry is important.

God proves His will (v13)

Paul builds this teaching not on his own opinion but on an historical fact. He points to those to whom God had given the baptism with the Holy Spirit and says that by giving the Spirit to certain groups of people, God had proven His will concerning His Church. Here's how he said that:

> "For indeed, in one Spirit we were all baptized [immersed] into one body, whether Jews or Greeks, whether slaves or free, and all were given one Spirit to drink" (1Co 12:13, literal).

In effect, Paul is looking back over the history of the church, beginning with Pentecost, and noting that God had given the Spirit to every ethnicity, religious background and social standing. On the day of Pentecost God brought into the church Jews from many different countries (Ac 2). When Philip went to Samaria, He brought in Samaritans (Ac 8). When Peter went to Caesarea, He brought in Romans (Ac 10, 11). When Paul went on his missionary journeys, He brought in Gentiles of all sorts. And when Paul came to Corinth most of those who flooded into the church were uneducated, poor and had no social position at all (1Co 1:26). Yet the one thing they did have, in addition to their faith in Jesus Christ, was the powerful arrival of the Holy Spirit. The Spirit, by baptizing them, by filling their "innermost being" with "rivers of living water" (Jn 7:38), had proven who it was that God welcomed into the church. It had been Jews and Greeks. It had been slaves and free. It had been men and women. It had been young and old. It had been barbarians and Scythians (Col 3:11). The same Holy Spirit was dwelling in all of them.

A recognizable reality

It's important to note that when Paul says that the baptism with the Holy Spirit proves that God accepts a wide variety of people into the Church, he is not pointing to something that is only a theological truth. He's pointing to a recognizable reality. In the early church the power of the Holy Spirit was so strong that people were receiving it easily. And what they received was observable. Something obviously happened when they were baptized with the Holy Spirit (Gordon Fee, God's Empowering Presence, Baker Academic, 1994, p.181). It was because the churches in Galatia had received "an experiential and visibly manifest reception of the Spirit" (Fee, p.181) that Paul could argue that his gospel of grace had been proven to be true. Listen:

> "You foolish Galatians, who has bewitched you, before whose eyes Jesus Christ was publicly portrayed as crucified? This is the only thing I want to find out from you: did you receive the Spirit by the works of the Law, or by hearing with faith? ...So then, does He who provides you with the Spirit and works miracles among you, do it by works of the Law, or by hearing with faith?" (Gal 3:1-5).

He was able to point to their common experience of receiving the Spirit as proof that God agreed with the gospel he had preached to them.

So it's God who decides who belongs in the church, not us. And Paul tells the Corinthians that we need only to look at those the Lord baptized with the Holy Spirit to discover what a wide variety of people that is. But in saying that, we need to insert a note of caution. Paul never meant to say that people who have not had a dramatic baptism with the Holy Spirit or don't speak with tongues are not full members of the Lord's Church. He would have been shocked that we had even asked him that question and would have quickly reminded us that it is by faith alone that a person becomes part of God's family. But when Paul wrote those statements, the early church was not arguing over the nature of the baptism with the Holy Spirit. Everyone assumed that what happened at Pentecost was still available (Ac 11:15-18). And the church deliberately helped people receive the gift of the Spirit that they had been given when they believed, so it was a normal part of their experience. If we, today, will again recognize the importance of receiving what we have been given, the same life of the Spirit that we read about in Corinth or Galatia will become a common, observable reality among us as well.

The Body of Christ (vs12-27)

The great family that Jesus has redeemed is very diverse. It's made up of many different types of people who have been called to function in many different ways. This diversity is not an accident; it is intentional. In order for the church to perform the full range of ministries that Jesus desires to do in a particular community, He gives different people different assignments and then asks them to support each other and work together in harmony. When that happens, that family of believers, the church in that location, can be compared to a human body. Just as our bodies have different organs that are designed to do different functions, some in the church are called to lead, others to follow; some do ministries that by their nature draw attention to the person doing it, others work behind the scenes and for that reason might be overlooked. That's why Paul says we must be diligent to view these various ministries the way God sees them: like different organs of the human body. Every organ is needed. Every organ performs a vital function. If any member of the human body were missing, that body would be limited in its activity or unable to survive. So is the church of Jesus Christ.

In this passage Paul is teaching us to think a certain way when we consider the Lord's church. He wants us to celebrate the diversity God sends, not reject it. No one should feel inferior or think of others as inferior. He wants us to see ourselves as a team and understand our role as a part of that team.

Recognizing the call (v27)

Paul closes this section with this summary statement:

> "Now you are Christ's body, and individually members of it" (1Co 12:27).

His point is unmistakable: Each of us has a role to play in the work Jesus wants to do in our community. Not only does the Holy Spirit care for each of us (vs7-11), but the Lord Jesus also calls each of us to minister on His behalf. And as Paul has shown us so clearly in this passage, all of us are needed, and all of us will be given different assignments. But the question that arises in many of us after listening to him is this: How do I know what I'm called to do? What is my place in His Body? Am I a hand or foot, or an ear or eye? How will I know? And of course, there are all sorts of answers that have been given to that question, but I think the first step toward the answer is very simple. I believe that if each of us will look within our heart and reflect on where God has given us a special compassion, we will be headed in the right direction. As Paul will teach us in the next chapter (1Co 13), the Lord always leads us by love. He guides us by love, not by ambition or guilt. Yes, as followers of Jesus Christ we are told to love all people, but no one can minister to all people. Each of us is only capable of being one part of the Body. So it seems the Lord places a very specific compassion for a very specific area of human need inside each of us. Certain kinds of needs will catch our eye. Certain types of suffering will persistently disturb us. Certain problems will cause us to wonder why someone isn't doing something about that. And it's likely that we've felt those feelings over the course of our lifetime. If we look back on our history, we will soon recognize a pattern of concern. Whenever we encountered that type of need, we felt an impulse to help. The Lord Jesus taught a parable that shows us someone who ministered to someone in need because they felt compassion. Listen to what He said about the Good Samaritan:

> "But a Samaritan, who was on a journey, came upon him; and when he saw him, he felt compassion, and came to him and bandaged up his wounds, pouring oil and wine on [them]; and he put him on his own beast, and brought him to an inn and took care of him" (Lk 10:33-34).

Two other travelers had already passed by this wounded man, but it was the Samaritan who stopped to help him because he felt compassion. And he not only helped the man in the moment, his compassion caused him to care for the man until he was well. Jesus concluded the story by saying that this Samaritan man had modeled what it means for us to love our neighbor as ourselves (Lk 10:27, 36). That makes the answer to the question, "How do I know what I'm called to do?" very simple. I need to recognize the areas of human need that stir my compassion and then watch for my "neighbor," and I will be well on my way to taking my place in the Body of Christ.

Chapter Fifteen

Guided by Love

27 Now you are Christ's body, and individually members of it. 28 And God has appointed in the church, first apostles, second prophets, third teachers, then miracles, then gifts of healings, helps, administrations, various kinds of tongues. 29 All are not apostles, are they? All are not prophets, are they? All are not teachers, are they? All are not workers of miracles, are they? 30 All do not have gifts of healings, do they? All do not speak with tongues, do they? All do not interpret, do they? 31 But earnestly desire the greater gifts. And I show you a still more excellent way. 13:1 If I speak with the tongues of men and of angels, but do not have love, I have become a noisy gong or a clanging cymbal. 2 If I have the gift of prophecy, and know all mysteries and all knowledge; and if I have all faith, so as to remove mountains, but do not have love, I am nothing. 3 And if I give all my possessions to feed the poor, and if I surrender my body to be burned, but do not have love, it profits me nothing.

1 Corinthians 12:27-13:3

A beautiful gift can be spoiled if it's given with a wrong attitude, and that's especially true when it comes to the gifts of the Spirit. Something that was pure and meant to heal, comfort or bring joy when it was sent from heaven can be delivered in such a way that it does just the opposite: It wounds, disturbs or leaves someone sad. Whatever comes from God is perfect (Jas 1:17), but He delivers His gifts through imperfect people, and that's where trouble can enter in. A human messenger can take a perfect gift and deliver it with anger, fear or pride. A messenger might "edit" a message by mixing some of God's words with some of their own until that message no longer resembles what God intended; it now says whatever the messenger wanted it to say.

When a person repents and places their faith in Jesus Christ, he or she becomes righteous before God, but that person's physical body, with its passions, appetites and subconscious attitudes, doesn't disappear. It still tries to influence everything we do, and it will continue to do that until we receive new, obedient bodies at the resurrection (Ro 8:23). Here's how Paul describes this tension between a believer's spirit and body:

> "If Christ is in you, though the body is dead because of sin, yet the spirit is alive because of righteousness" (Ro 8:10).

He pictures a renewed, human spirit living inside an old, rebellious body and says God gave us the Holy Spirit to provide the power we would need to put to death the deeds of that body (Ro 8:13). He's explaining to us why believers still have to wrestle with the passions and attitudes that come from their bodies. He says our "flesh" rebels against the ways of God (Ro 8:7). So if we're not careful, it can pollute everything we do, including the way we minister the gifts of the Spirit.

If you and I are going to deliver one of God's gifts, or receive a gift for ourselves, we must learn to recognize the difference between the voice of the Holy Spirit and the voice of our own flesh. We must learn to filter out wrong thoughts and pass on, or receive, only those we believe to be from the Lord, which raises the question: How do I know when God is guiding me to say or do something? And what sign should I look for that would alert me that a word or action is not from God but has been produced by my flesh? In this passage Paul answers those questions with one word: love. He tells the Corinthians: Check your heart before you say or do anything on God's behalf, and especially before you minister one of the "graces" of the Holy Spirit (charismata). If God is guiding you, you will feel His love for those to whom you are ministering, and that love will tell you when to speak or act and when to wait. It will control the tone and manner in which you do what you do. And Paul says these things using strong, beautiful language. His words leave no room for doubt: Without love, nothing we do pleases God.

So let's listen again to what he told the Corinthians, and then let's make a fresh commitment to let love guide us.

What did Paul say? (1Co 12:27-13:3)

These verses have been the subject of much controversy, and that should come as no surprise because they're usually translated in a way that makes them sound as if Paul suddenly contradicts himself. No sooner does he finish explaining that God places a wide variety of ministries in the Body of Christ, and that every member is vitally important to the success of the whole, then he seems to turn at verse 28 and rank those ministries and "graces" of the Spirit in a list that starts at the most important and runs down to the least important. Then, to make matters even worse, he seems to tell us to pursue only the ones at the top of the list ("the greater gifts") and ignore those at the bottom. And if that were what he actually said, then it would mean we should all try to be apostles, prophets or teachers. No one should desire to participate in lesser ministries like helps, administration or speaking in tongues. But thankfully, these verses can be translated in a manner that is consistent with what Paul taught earlier. Here is a careful paraphrase of these verses based on a literal translation. In other words, here's what I think the Corinthians heard Paul try to teach them:

12:27-28: And you Corinthians are a body of Christ. You are one congregation among all the many congregations around the world. So think of yourselves as Christ's body in that city. And because you are a body of Christ, all the principles I've been teaching you about the church being similar to a human body apply to you as well. If you look at what God has already done in Corinth, you will see that He has placed among you a wide variety of ministries. Just look at your history. First, He sent apostles to you. I was the apostle who founded that church (Ac 18:1-17), but Apollos and Peter came there as well (1Co 1:12; 3:6). Then He raised up men and women who were capable of bringing genuine prophecy so that through them He could edify, exhort and comfort you as needed (1Co 14:3). They were especially important in the early years because you did not have my letters or any other Christian Scriptures. And then thankfully, there were some learned Jews and proselytes in Corinth who became followers of Jesus so that after I left, there were teachers who could open the Old Testament and show you how Jesus fulfilled, or will fulfill, important prophesies about the Messiah and explain to you the mercy and holiness of the God of Israel. You were blessed with a number of teachers like Aquila and Priscilla (Ac 18:2; 1Co 16:19), Crispus (Ac 18:8; 1Co 1:14), Stephanas (1Co 1:16; 16:15), and Sosthenes (Ac 18:17; 1Co 1:1). Each of these had a solid background in the Bible and, therefore, were able to teach the large number of Greeks who flooded into the church. They kept everyone focused in the right direction.

So to those three ministries (apostles, prophets and teachers) God gave the greatest amount of authority and visibility, but He also placed other ministries among you that by their nature draw attention to those who perform them. For example, there are those who pray with great power and through their prayers see miracles and demonic deliverance take place, and those who minister healing to the sick. But just as a human body has organs that are not visible when you look at a person, yet those organs perform vital functions, God gives to the Body of Christ people who minister in ways that most of the church doesn't see. For example, there are those who care for widows and orphans, lead house churches or prayer meetings, powerfully intercede for others from the privacy of their own homes, or do the many hidden things that are necessary to prepare for special events.

In a similar way you will observe that God has placed a wide variety of ministries in your worship services. In any particular gathering the Holy Spirit distributes His "graces" to whomever He wishes. For example, He might ask two or three people to speak in tongues loud enough for everyone to hear (1Co 14:27).

12:29-30: God didn't appoint everyone in the church to be an apostle or a prophet, even though everyone is capable of bringing a prophecy when God asks them to do so (1Co 14:1, 5, 24, 31). He didn't appoint everyone to be a teacher, though hopefully in time all of you will grow to the point where you are able to teach others (Heb 5:12). Nor does everyone in the church see amazing miracles or healings take place when they pray, though Jesus promised that potential to all of us (Mk 11:22-24; Jn 14:12). And during a particular worship service God doesn't ask everyone to pray or praise aloud in a language they never learned. In fact, there should never be more than two or three such expressions in any one service (1Co 14:27). Nor does He ask everyone to interpret what was said in those unknown languages (1Co 14:14-17).

12:31: As I mentioned to you in the opening to this letter (1Co 1:7), you Corinthians have all the "graces" of the Spirit (Greek: charismata) being expressed in your services, but the attitude in which you minister is very wrong. You jealously compete with one another trying to be the person who brings the most impressive manifestation ("the greater charismata"). And though I am glad that you are zealous for the things of the Spirit, I'm now going to point out to you a much better way of deciding how and when to participate in these "graces." I don't want you to be guided by pride or competitiveness anymore.

13:1-3: The better way I want to show you all comes down to identifying your motive. Ask yourself: Why am I doing what I am doing? Because if your motive is right, God will be pleased, but if it's wrong, whatever you do will be of no spiritual benefit to you at all. And the only right motive for doing any form of ministry is that God's selfless love impels you to serve that person or group. No matter how spiritual or dramatic a manifestation may be, if it is not done with the right attitude, it is spiritually worthless, at least as far as you are concerned. Even if others are helped, God knows why you did what you did, and He's not pleased because His goal for you is that you become like Jesus (Ro 8:29), and what you are doing isn't like Jesus at all. This is true for all the "graces" of the Spirit whether it be tongues, prophecy, profound words of knowledge or miracle-producing prayers of faith. It's even true of extravagant giving or martyrdom. In other words, everything a believer does in ministry must be motivated and guided by love. When you're alone, you can focus on edifying yourself (1Co 14:4 5, 18-19), but when other people are involved, don't say anything or do anything until you feel God's love for them, and He shows you when and how to help them.

Why love?

Throughout this passage Paul is talking about one particular kind of love. The Greek word he uses is "agape." It points to the selfless kind of love that Jesus modeled for us in everything He did, but above all when He willingly died on the cross. That kind of love is not based on an emotion; it's based on the choice someone makes to lay aside their own rights and needs and to care for the needs of others. And as we've heard today, Paul made an astounding claim about the attitude we must have if we are going to minister to anyone. He said unless this Christ-like love is present in us and guides us to do whatever we do, God considers our words and actions worthless in terms of His goal for our lives. Loveless ministry shows that we are personally headed in the wrong direction. We're becoming less like Jesus, not more like Him. And God's primary concern for you and me is to conform us, to work inside us, until we genuinely have a heart like Jesus'. Listen:

> "For those whom He foreknew, He also predestined [to become] conformed to the image of His Son, so that He would be the firstborn among many brethren" (Ro 8:29).

Paul is telling us that before God created the universe, He saw everything that would happen. He knew Adam and Eve would sin, but He also knew that in every generation there would be men and women of faith who would repent and trust Him to give them mercy. And He decided, way back then, before Creation, to send His Son to save those people and to send the Holy Spirit to change their hearts until there would be billions of people as pure and loving as His beautiful Son. And He also decided this: that someday He would resurrect them, and they would shine with His glory, just like His Son.

Now, if that's God's goal for us, if that's our destiny, then trying to compete with one another or proudly displaying how spiritual we are completely misses the point. What matters, what lasts, is the Christ-like love that's being formed inside us.

Chapter Sixteen

The Spirit's Assignment

[4]Love is patient, love is kind and is not jealous; love does not brag and is not arrogant, [5]does not act unbecomingly; it does not seek its own, is not provoked, does not take into account a wrong suffered, [6]does not rejoice in unrighteousness, but rejoices with the truth; [7]bears all things, believes all things, hopes all things, endures all things.

1 Corinthians 13:4-7

The most important role of the Holy Spirit, the primary reason the Father sent Him to us through the Son, is to make us holy, not to make us powerful. Frequently when people talk about the coming of the Spirit, they say He has come to equip us for service. In their minds He is basically the "Giver of all gifts." He's the One who empowers us to do ministry more effectively. And that's true; He is the "Giver of all gifts," but that's not His most important role. Others say He is the great Teacher, that His assignment is to lead us into all truth (Jn 16:13), which in their minds means He will help us understand biblical passages that speak about Jesus. And that's also true. He is the "Spirit of Truth" who teaches us all things and brings to remembrance all that Jesus said (Jn 14:26). But the giving of knowledge isn't His most important assignment either, not if we believe what Paul says in this portion of his letter to the Corinthians. Paul says the most important thing in our lives isn't power, and it isn't knowledge. It isn't deeds of any kind, not even deeds of great generosity or courage. It's having our heart changed to become like Jesus' heart. So again, the most important role of the Holy Spirit is to make us holy, which is another way of saying to make us like Jesus. And above all else that means to love like He loves, or maybe it would be better to say, to be filled with His love.

Paul's description of love in this passage is a description of the character of God. When the apostle John writes "God is love" (1Jn 4:8), he's telling us that everything God does is ultimately an expression of His love. Love is why He made us. Love is why He sent His Son to save us. Love is why He disciplines us, and love is even why He will someday judge the world in righteousness. From the foundation of the world it has been the Father's plan that we will become like His Son. That doesn't mean that we will cease to have our own personalities, but it does mean everything we do will be done because we love Him with all our heart, mind and soul, and our neighbor as ourselves (Mk 12:30-31; Ro 13:9; Gal 5:14; Jas 2:8). It means that these characteristics of love that Paul pictures so beautifully not only describe our Lord, they will ultimately describe you and me. This is the way we will love when our heavenly Father has finished conforming us into the image of His Son (Ro 8:29).

What love does (1Co 13:4-7)

It's enlightening to note that Paul describes love by what it does, not by how it feels. In these four verses he lists 15 actions to which our decision to love others with God's kind of love will lead us. Here is a brief description of each:

13:4: The first thing love does is to suffer long. This is the literal meaning of what is usually translated as "love is patient." A person with this kind of love is able to endure hardship or mistreatment while waiting for God to accomplish His purpose in the beloved. It "buys time" for God to do His work in a person or a situation (In dangerous situations or with dangerous people this patient waiting may need to be done at a safe distance). Next, love is kind. To be kind is to mercifully help someone in need. Jesus' parable about the Good Samaritan is an illustration of kindness. A traveling Samaritan stopped to care for an injured man. He dressed his wounds, carried him to an inn and even paid for his stay while he recuperated. Jesus used this parable to explain what it meant to "love your neighbor as yourself" (Lk 10:27-37). This type of practical service is what Paul means when he says "love is kind." God's love doesn't just sit there; it gets up and does something to help. Next, love is not jealous. People who act out of Christ-like love do so because they love God and want to let His love reach others through them. Their attitude tends to honor others and bring peace. This is very different from those whose motivation is to prove that they are as good as or better than someone else. The word we translate here as "jealous" describes people who are competing with one another. And that kind of competition results in someone becoming either a winner or a loser; it produces either shame or pride (1Co 3:3). Next, love does not brag. The word Paul uses pictures someone who "parades" in front of others. He's telling us that those who are motivated by love don't do things in order to draw attention to themselves, and they don't take credit for the good things God accomplishes through them (1Co 1:31). They acknowledge their absolute dependence on God and marvel at the fact that God would be willing to use someone like them. Next, love is not arrogant. Paul literally says "love is not puffed up." He pictures someone puffed out like a pair of billows with their own self-importance. The word can be applied to those who push into a position of leadership to which God has not called them, and there was much of that kind of striving for prominence taking place in Corinth (1Co 4:6-8). It revealed hearts that lacked the Christ-like love which regards another as more important than oneself (Php 2:3). A loving person seeks to serve; an arrogant person seeks to be admired.

13:5: Next, love does not act unbecomingly. The person who loves with God's kind of love does not intentionally do things that might embarrass or offend others. There may be times when God asks us to minister in a bold way that might embarrass certain people, but that's not the kind of offense to which Paul is referring. He's talking about individuals who selfishly ignore accepted patterns of behavior or dress because they don't care what others think (1Co 10:32, 33). Next, love does not seek its own. Christ-like love is focused outward, away from self. Paul's purpose is not to point us toward a life of self-neglect, but he's cautioning those who greedily pursue spiritual blessings for themselves, reminding them that God's love will always lead them toward a life of serving others. Very shortly he will give us a practical illustration of how this selflessness controls the use of the "graces" of the Spirit in a church gathering (1Co 14:4-5, 18-19). Next Paul states that love is not provoked. The selfless focus of God's love protects a person from being easily angered and drawn into heated arguments. Preserving relationships becomes more important than demanding one's rights or winning an argument. Next, love does not take into account a wrong suffered. The person who loves with Christ-like love does not keep a mental record of the bad things that have been done to him or her, or find comfort in the hope that someday an opportunity will come to settle the score. God's love longs to win the lost and heal the broken, so its concern is to see that person's life grow spiritually rather than waiting to get even with them.

13:6: Next, love does not rejoice in unrighteousness. The person who loves is never happy to hear that another person has done something foolish or fallen morally. He or she won't laugh when they hear that someone has stumbled or enjoy gossiping about the ungodly things that were done (Ro 1:32; 1Co 5:1-2). Instead, love rejoices with the truth. It longs to see others do that which pleases God so that every possible person will go to heaven and be rewarded by Christ for their faithfulness. It rejoices in knowing that God rejoices when people draw close to Him.

13:7: Next, love bears all things. The Greek word Paul uses here actually means to cover something by putting a roof over it, and I think what he is saying is that when love sees unrighteousness (v6), it seeks to cover that person's sin by not exposing it to those who don't need to know. In a sense it protects that person from being publicly shamed (Ge 9:20-23). Next, love believes all things. Because love longs to help those in need, it aggressively lays hold of all of God's promises. It seeks to grow in faith in order to release healing or drive back demonic attack. It believes everything the Bible says about God loving the lost, forgiving the repentant and providing eternal life. So it fights for the beloved by laying hold of God's promises on their behalf. Next, love hopes all things. Biblical hope is the confidence that good things will happen in the future because God is at work in the present. Since agape love flows out of the realization of all God has done for us, it keeps a person optimistic that sooner or later God will transform a beloved's heart or act powerfully on their behalf. Love keeps expecting God to win, and that hope sustains us as we pour ourselves out on behalf of others. And finally, love endures all things. One would think that by loving this way we would run out of love, our supply of love would become exhausted, but that's not the case. We soon find that there is a miraculous quality to God's love: The more love we give, the more love we have. The process itself expands our capacity to love rather than diminishing it. So when Paul says love endures all things, he means nothing can quench it. It doesn't die out with the passing of time, nor do we run dry when we include more people. Instead, it grows until it becomes a way of life.

The source of love

When we come to the end of Paul's description of what love does, it would be hard for anyone to say that the love he pictures isn't absolutely wonderful. Who wouldn't want to be loved like that, and who wouldn't want to love others that way? But this type of love isn't commonly found in the human heart, so it feels like a distant ideal that we would all like to reach for but should never expect to achieve. And apart from a miracle I think agape love, Christ-like love, is an unreachable prize. Yet Paul did expect it. He wrote these words because he wanted us to love like that. So what is the source of such love because it's not normally found in humans? And that question brings us back to the Holy Spirit.

Here's a simple definition of God's kind of love: It's the decision to do whatever it takes to save someone. The Bible tells us that it was His love that led God to make the decision to do what had to be done to bring as many people to heaven as possible. Jesus explained it this way:

> "For God so loved the world, that He gave His only begotten Son, that whoever believes in Him shall not perish, but have eternal life" (Jn 3:16).

In other words, the Father's love produced the decision to send His Son to the cross, and I believe that statement points to the source that enables us to love that way as well.

Paul has shown us in this passage that there is a dimension of love far more selfless and long-lasting than anything the human heart can produce by itself. He has described something that can only be based on a miracle. It must be a gift God places, by the Holy Spirit, into the human heart. You might say He takes a portion of His own love and puts it inside us. And as you would expect, His love makes us do things we would never do without it. The closest thing to God's love that the human heart can produce by itself is what we might call heroic love. In certain situations some people will literally choose to lay down their life to protect others. We see this with soldiers in battle protecting a comrade, police defending the innocent, firefighters rescuing the helpless, or a parent defending a child in danger. And it's very beautiful when it happens, so we naturally honor it because in that moment that heroic love is a picture of God saving us (Jn 15:13). But when God places His love inside someone, heroic love becomes a lifestyle.

Through the prophet Ezekiel God promised that after His Son died and rose again from the dead, He would miraculously transform the hearts of those who received the new covenant. Listen:

> "Moreover, I will give you a new heart and put a new spirit within you; and I will remove the heart of stone from your flesh and give you a heart of flesh" (Eze 36:26).

As you can see, God was promising to do something new, something humans couldn't produce by their own efforts, something so radical it would be like taking out a dead, stony heart and putting in a warm, living heart. And unless we understand this miracle, we won't understand what Paul is saying. We'll think he's describing an unreachable ideal, a distant goal to be admired but never achieved. But he's not. He's describing the love that moved the Father to send Jesus into the world and the love that moved Jesus to choose the cross. And he's describing the love that is already present inside of you and me if we have become children of God (Jn 1:12-13). If we are God's children, then He has put a portion of His own heart within us. He has made it possible for us to love like He loves. It's no longer a remote goal; it has become an immediate possibility. It's not a vague ideal; it's the ability to do what we promised Jesus we would do when we said we would take up our cross and follow Him (Lk 9:23).

Chapter Seventeen

Love Never Falls

[8]Love never fails; but if there are gifts of prophecy, they will be done away; if there are tongues, they will cease; if there is knowledge, it will be done away. [9]For we know in part and we prophesy in part; [10]but when the perfect comes, the partial will be done away. [11]When I was a child, I used to speak like a child, think like a child, reason like a child; when I became a man, I did away with childish things. [12]For now we see in a mirror dimly, but then face to face; now I know in part, but then I will know fully just as I also have been fully known. [13]But now faith, hope, love, abide these three; but the greatest of these is love.

1 Corinthians 13:8-13

No matter how old you are, your life is just beginning. What we do in this lifetime matters a great deal because it affects our future. The physical death of our body is not the end of our service to God. Initially our human spirit will be caught up into His presence and joined with those believers who have arrived there before us. During that time we will be clothed in a spiritual body, not a physical body, but our existence in that condition will only be temporary. What most people call "heaven" is not our final destination. It's the place we go if we die before the next age arrives. It's a joyful time of waiting for our resurrection.

In this chapter of his letter to the Corinthians Paul reminds us that another age of earth's history will follow this one, and all of us who believe in Jesus

Christ will be part of that age. When the time allotted for this age comes to an end, the Father will give the order, and all who belong to Him, both the living and the dead, will be resurrected into immortal bodies. Then, in that new immortal condition we will return to the earth with Jesus to extend His ministry to the billions of people still alive after the natural catastrophes of the great tribulation and the battle of Armageddon. And then you and I will step into an area of ministry assigned to us by the Lord. At that moment all the godly character and wisdom that had been worked into us during this lifetime will become an important foundation for the ministries we will be asked to perform in that new season. So the faithfulness we've shown here is a factor that determines the initial amount of ministry we will be assigned there (Mt 19:27-30; 25:14-30; Lk 16:10-12; 19:11-27; 1Co 3:13-15). That means believers should think of this age as a training ground for the far more intense level of ministry that we will be doing in the next age. Yet even the next age, which the Bible says will last a thousand years, is <u>not</u> the final age. At the end of that thousand-year period of time every part of this present universe will disappear, and God will create a new heaven and a new earth (Rev 21).

And this amazing future that lies before us, of one age following upon another, isn't mere speculation. It's what Jesus taught. It's what Paul taught. It's what the prophets of Israel taught. And it is this understanding that lies behind Paul's words about love that we are reading in this passage today. This is the future that God has planned for us, and it explains why faith, hope and love abide, and it explains why love is greater than faith and hope. It's a future you and I need to see because it will change the way we live here and now.

Love never falls (1Co 13:8-13)

After describing the various activities to which God's kind of love leads us (vs4-7), Paul concludes his list with one final statement. He says, "Love never <u>falls</u>" (literal, Greek: pipto). What he wrote is usually translated as "Love never <u>fails</u>," but He actually said, "Love never <u>falls</u>." And I believe Paul choses that word to assure us that love will never fall from its position of prominence. It is the one quality of heart that makes us the most like Jesus. It's the quality that gives our heavenly Father the greatest delight when He sees it formed in us. And as Paul is about to explain, it is a quality that, when it has been formed in us, becomes part of us forever. Here's my understanding of these verses in which Paul explains why love never falls but the grace-gifts of the Spirit (charismata) will:

13:8: He says in the age to come prophecies will be brought to a state of inactivity, and undoubtedly that is because God will be speaking directly to His people. Speaking in tongues will cease because people will no longer need to use that gift. After the resurrection their fleshly mind will no longer exist, and therefore, there will be nothing to hinder what their renewed human spirit wants to say to God. And the [word of] knowledge will also be brought to a state of inactivity because we will "know fully" just as we "have been fully known" (v12).

13:9: Paul says the grace-gifts of the Spirit at work in this present age are "partial." Of course, he does not mean by that statement that they are imperfect in any way, but that they are incomplete. Because of our limited spiritual capacity we now tend to receive only part of all God wants to give us.

13:10: But in the age to come there will be no barrier between the resurrected children of God and God Himself. In this age we need all the grace-gifts to help us overcome the limitations of our not-yet redeemed body (Ro 8:23, 26). But those gifts won't be needed after we've been resurrected, and our rebellious flesh is gone, after Satan has been bound (Rev 20:1-3), after Jesus has physically returned, and after the Holy Spirit has "baptized" the whole earth with His presence like the waters cover the sea (Isa 11:9; Hab 2:14).

13:11: The difference between the way we are now and the way we will be then is like the difference between a child and an adult. Our minds, then, will be taught by the Lord. They will be free from the restrictions that deceive or confuse us. We will think with perfect clarity. Our rebellious flesh will be gone. Our subconscious mind will be free of sorrow, regret and crippling memories. Old behaviors and attitudes that were produced by the influence of our flesh will have come to an end. Our redeemed spirit will rule our body, and that body will have no rebellion in it.

13:12: Right now our communication with God is hindered. What we see and know of Him can be clouded by misinformation and doubt. But when Jesus comes again, we will be able to talk directly to Him. When we've put on our "spiritual" bodies (1Co 15:44), we will be able to walk with Him and speak with Him as Adam and Eve did in the garden of Eden before they sinned (Ge 3:8). We will speak to Him "face to face" as Abraham and Sarah did when they served Him dinner at Hebron (Ge 18:1-2), or as Moses did when the pillar of cloud stood before the door of the tent of meeting (Ex 33:11; Dt 34:10). Then there will no longer be a barrier between us and our heavenly Father or between us and our Lord Jesus. The Bible tells us that Jesus will be physically present, ruling the earth from Jerusalem, and that we will be His deputies extending His ministry and authority to the mortal humans still living on the planet. In that new resurrected condition we will fully realize what it means to be "children of God." We behold and understand Him as freely as He beholds and understands us.

13:13: The dramatic contrast between our relationship with God in this age and our relationship with Him in the next raises an obvious question: What qualities does He want to work into our character now because they will go with us into the next age? And in this verse Paul answers that question. He says there are three which will be needed in the next age as much as they are now. They are faith, hope and love, and of these three, he says love is the greatest.

Faith and hope

It's easier to understand how love will play a part in the next age than it is to understand why faith and hope will be needed. When we are able to communicate "face to face" with God, why would we need faith? If we have already been resurrected, why would we need hope? What promises would we be waiting for God to fulfill? What future blessings would be missing? The answer, particularly if a person wrongly assumes that their final destination is heaven, might surprise us. If we read the Bible carefully, we will discover that the "age to come," the one that immediately follows this present age, is <u>not</u> the final age. There will be another age beyond that one, one which will be filled with a level of glory even greater than the glory that will fill the thousand-year age that lies directly ahead of us. John, in the book of <u>Revelation</u>, calls it "a new heaven and a new earth" (Rev 21:1). And that truth about that <u>ultimate</u> future is the key that unlocks our understanding of what Paul means when he says, "But now faith, hope, love, abide these three; but the greatest of these is love" (1Co 13:13). It explains why there will still be a need for faith and hope during the Millennium, the Messianic Age, the "age to come." During that thousand-year period of time we will exercise hope because we will be waiting for promises that have not yet arrived. Though we, believers, will already have been resurrected, an un-resurrected human population and the animal world will still be aging and dying (Isa 65:20). The devil, though bound for a season, will not have been removed forever. The new heaven and earth will not have been created. And though we will never die, we will be ministering to people who are dying, so on their behalf we will be laying hold of God's promises and looking forward to the end of death. In other words, faith and hope will still be part of our walk with God. That's why Paul says they "abide" (remain). They continue on past this age into the next. And then even the next age will pass away, and an entirely new universe will take its place. At last, you and I will be living in a city lighted by the glory of God and the Lamb (Rev 21:23), and the Lord God Almighty and the Lamb will be our temple (Rev 21:22). At last, in that final age, there will be no more need for faith or hope because all the promises will have arrived in full. Yet our need for love in the New Jerusalem will not have diminished at all. Surely we will still be loving God and each other far more than we do now. That's why Paul can declare so boldly, "love never falls!"

An eternal perspective

Paul is telling the Corinthian church that the grace-gifts of the Holy Spirit are important, and he wants them to passionately pursue those gifts, but he also wants them to remember what is most important. And what's most important, more important than even the use of the gifts, is that their heart be conformed to the heart of Jesus. So he puts the gifts of the Spirit into perspective by reminding them that these "partial" gifts will only be used in this age, not in the next. In the next there will be perfect communication with God and an availability of His power that is vastly beyond anything we experience now. But the Christ-like character that's formed in us now will still be at work in us then. In the next age we will still be waiting in hope for the new heaven and earth, and we will still need faith because we will be ministering to people who are subject to sin and decay. But in time that age will also pass away, and the one quality we can carry with us into the eternal glory of the new heaven and earth will be love. So the more we love, the more we become like Jesus, and the more we become like Jesus, the more we approach God's predestined plan for us (Ro 8:29).

What would love do?

Paul wanted the Corinthians to use this truth to evaluate everything they were doing. In effect, he wanted them to ask themselves: What would love do? Would it march into the pagan temples and eat in the idol feasts regardless of the grief that it caused a brother or sister who had recently escaped the grip of that demonic religion? (1Co 8). Would it gorge itself on the bread or get drunk on the wine served in the Lord's Supper while poorer members of the church sat outside with nothing to eat or drink? (1Co 11:17-34). Would it speak in tongues loudly and all at once ignoring the confusion that behavior caused the visitors who had come to hear about Jesus? (1Co 14:20-25). Would it conduct side conversations during church services that distracted those who were trying to worship? (1Co 14:34-35). And, of course, the answer to each of these questions is no. So what would love do? It would set aside its own freedoms, if necessary, to protect the faith of a weaker believer. It would see that every believer participated in the Lord's Supper and give what was left over to the poor to take home with them. It would spend a great deal of time speaking in tongues privately, but in a public service it would seek to express the gifts in such a way that they draw others closer to God. It would avoid doing anything in a service that might draw the congregation's attention away from Jesus.

Paul's counsel was not just meant for the church in Corinth; it was also meant for the church in every generation. He wants us to understand that the Holy Spirit has not only come to equip us for the present but to prepare us for the future. And above all else, He has come to teach us to love like Jesus loves because that kind of love will never fall.

Chapter Eighteen

Learning to Prophesy

[1]Pursue love, yet desire earnestly spiritual gifts, but especially that you may prophesy. [2]For one who speaks in a tongue does not speak to men but to God; for no one understands, but in his spirit he speaks mysteries. [3]But one who prophesies speaks to men for edification and exhortation and consolation. [4]One who speaks in a tongue edifies himself; but one who prophesies edifies the church. [5]Now I wish that you all spoke in tongues, but even more that you would prophesy; and greater is one who prophesies than one who speaks in tongues, unless he interprets, so that the church may receive edifying.[6]But now, brethren, if I come to you speaking in tongues, what will I profit you unless I speak to you either by way of revelation or of knowledge or of prophecy or of teaching?

1 Corinthians 14:1-6

Moses longed for it to happen (Nu 11:29); the prophet Joel said it would happen (Joel 2:28-29), and on the day of Pentecost the apostle Peter said it had finally arrived (Ac 2:16): God gave the gift of prophecy to every one of His people, men and women, young and old. Throughout Israel's history there had always been prophets, but they were very special individuals and quite rare. Their assignment was to remind the nation of the covenants God had made with them through Abraham (Ge 15:4-21), Moses at Mount Sinai (Ex 24:4-8) and David (2Sa 7:4-17). They warned them that disobedience would bring the curses written in the Law of Moses (Dt 28:15-68) and promised them that obedience would bring the blessings (Dt 28:1-14).

Their counsel was seldom followed during their lifetime, but because what they said would happen actually did happen, their writings were preserved as Scripture, and future generations were able to look back and recognize that God had spoken through them. The Bible says Abraham was a prophet (Ge 20:7; Ps 105:15); Moses was a prophet (Dt 18:15-19; 34:10), and even David was a prophet (Mt 22:43; Ac 2:29-30). It was a person's capacity to hear from the Lord and then faithfully communicate to others what God had said that made that person a true prophet. And the standard was high: one wrong statement and that person was considered a false prophet (Dt 18:20-22). But that line of Old Testament prophets finally came to an end. John the Baptist was the last one (Mt 11:13). That's why the apostle John is so careful to record exactly what John the Baptist said about Jesus (Jn 1:6-8, 15, 19-36; 3:23-36). In effect, here was the last, great spokesman for the covenants declaring that God had shown him that Jesus was the Messiah for whom they had all been waiting. It was time for the New Covenant to arrive.

What Jesus did on the cross and by His resurrection profoundly changed the way human beings are able to relate to God. He made it possible for the Holy Spirit to dwell inside our physical bodies just as He dwelt inside the tabernacle in the wilderness or the temple in Jerusalem. Now, as Jeremiah prophesied would happen, every believer can have a deep, personal relationship with God. Listen:

> "They shall not teach again, each man his neighbor and each man his brother, saying, 'Know the Lord,' for they shall all know Me, from the least of them to the greatest of them… for I will forgive their iniquity, and their sin I will remember no more" (Jer 31:34).

Through Jeremiah the Lord promised that He would make a New Covenant that would apply to every one of His people, from the least to the greatest. And for those who have received this New Covenant, everything has changed, including the role of prophets. That special and rare individual, upon whom the Holy Spirit rested to empower him or her to remind Israel of covenants made with their ancestors, has been replaced by all of God's people, each one a living temple of the Holy Spirit empowered to proclaim the blessings of the New Covenant that God has now made available to the entire world through Jesus Christ (Heb 8:6-13).

This shift from a few to all is an essential element in Joel's prophecy about God's restoration of His people in the last days. Listen:

> "'And it shall be in the last days,' God says, 'that I will pour forth of My Spirit on all mankind, and your sons and your daughters shall prophesy, and your young men shall see visions, and your old men shall dream dreams; even on My bondslaves, both men and women, I will in those days pour forth of My Spirit and they shall prophesy'" (Ac 2:17-18).

And all of this is associated with the coming of the Messiah (Isa 11), so Peter meant exactly what he said when he stood up before that large crowd on the day of Pentecost and announced that the fulfillment of Joel's prophecy had begun that day. Jesus, the Messiah, had come. His death on the cross had removed the barrier of our sins, and His resurrection had proven that fact. Then, as the ascended Lord, He had sent the Holy Spirit to dwell inside every man, woman and child who was willing to repent and believe in Him (Ac 2:38-39). From that moment on not only could all prophesy, all could do every type of ministry that Jesus had done (Jn 14:12).

Understanding the change

Unless you and I understand the profound change that has taken place because of the New Covenant, we will find ourselves drifting back into Old-Covenant thinking. If we lose sight of the indwelling presence that Jesus' sacrifice on the cross made possible (Rom 8:3-4), in other words, if we don't realize what happens when someone is baptized with the Holy Spirit, we will forget that the Giver of all gifts dwells within us. We will sit back and wait passively for a few special people to tell us what God says.

Most believers need to be taught that they can prophesy. The thought of speaking the word of the Lord can be so intimidating that many of us become afraid to step out and try. And frankly, few of us know anyone who is able to teach us how to properly minister in this gift. So when we read passages in the Bible that indicate that we can all prophesy, we might acknowledge that those statements are true but still have a very hard time acknowledging that they are true for us. We simply don't know where to start. We think to ourselves, "Maybe the Spirit will come upon me so strongly someday that

I will helplessly blurt out the word God wants me to say. But until then, I don't want to say anything at all because I might say something wrong." That cautious attitude is certainly better than being unconcerned as to whether our words are from God or not. But our only options aren't silence or recklessness. There is a way to learn how to prophesy. In a healthy church there will be people who know Scripture soundly enough to help us evaluate the authenticity of what we believe we are hearing (1Co 14:29). So if we're brave enough to try and humble enough to be corrected, we will in time learn to discern the source behind what we're hearing or seeing and be able to test for ourselves if a particular statement or vision is in agreement with Scripture. Then, with practice we can let God speak through us whenever He wants to.

Listening to Paul (1Co 14:1-6)

Before we look at some practical steps that can help us learn to prophesy, let's listen to some of what Paul said about the importance of prophecy in his letter to the Corinthians. I've paraphrased these six verses so he can teach us as freely as he taught them. Here's what I hear Paul saying:

> "Now that you understand what real love is and why it is so important that you allow it to guide you in everything you do, I'm going to show you how God's love can guide you in the use of the grace-gifts of the Spirit. I'll use speaking in tongues and prophecy as my examples. Let me be clear: I don't want you to stop being passionate for the things of the Spirit. What I'm trying to teach you is that you must always let love guide you in how and when you minister in the Spirit. In the past your passion was focused on speaking in tongues, but in the future when you gather as a church, I want you to seek to prophesy rather than to speak out in tongues so loud that everyone can hear you because the person who speaks in tongues is speaking only to God since no one else knows what he or she is saying. Their words are a mystery to those who hear them. Yes, the person who is speaking in that unknown language is being personally edified, but in a church service that's not enough. We have to consider the needs of those around us. When God's love is guiding us, we no longer focus on ourselves but rather on how we can help others (1Co 13:5). So when you gather, please

understand that prophecy is of far greater value than tongues because when someone prophesies, everyone either has their faith strengthened or their will challenged to take a step of obedience or their heart comforted by God's promises.

"Don't misunderstand me: I am not telling you to stop speaking in tongues. In fact, I want all of you to speak in tongues, but when you gather with others, I want you to ask the Lord to show you how you can be of help to the whole congregation. And if you'll do that, when it comes to a choice between speaking in tongues in the service or prophesying, you'll choose to prophesy because that gift will help someone else. The exception to that rule would be if God specifically asked you to speak out in a tongue and told you that He would also give you the interpretation afterward, so you could explain to everyone what was said. In that case the whole church would be blessed by the beautiful prayer or praise that your human spirit spoke to God in a foreign language (1Co 14:13-17). When God tells you to bring a tongue and interpret it so it can be heard by all, the interpretation is just as edifying to the church, in its own way, as a prophecy.

"Here's an illustration that will help you understand what I mean. Imagine what would happen if I (Paul) came to Corinth, and all I did was speak to you in tongues. You wouldn't understand a word I'd said, and I wouldn't have helped you at all. But I would never do that because I love you. I'm not going to spend my time among you edifying myself. I'm going to speak the word of the Lord to you in your own language so I can edify you. When I'm with you, I want to uncover passages in the Bible about Jesus that you didn't understand, or help you discern the will of the Lord for you in a particular situation, or prophesy so you can see how God's promises apply to whatever need you have, or teach you how to function as a disciple of Jesus Christ. You see, my love for you will always cause me to ask God for a gift that will help you, one that you can understand and receive. And your love for one another should do the same" (paraphrase).

Learning to prophesy

So Paul not only wants all of us to speak in tongues, he wants all of us to prophesy, and as we've seen, that is exactly what we should expect if we've entered into the New Covenant. But if we've never learned to prophesy, Paul's encouraging words remain only a distant ideal. Though the Bible does not specifically teach us how to do this, here are several steps, based on what I've learned over the years, that I believe will help anyone who has received the baptism with the Holy Spirit to step out into the gift of prophecy:

1. Learn the character of God. By continually reading the Bible a person learns to answer the important question, "Would God say that?" Only when we know Scripture and are submitted to Scripture are we safe to prophesy (1Co 14:37-38).

2. Learn the voice of God. By meditating on passages of Scripture until you receive inspiration, you'll learn to recognize the difference between your own thoughts and God's thoughts. You'll learn what it feels like when God reveals a truth.

3. Learn the voice of your flesh. By trial and error with honest self-evaluation, you can learn from your successes and your mistakes. You will learn to question the source behind what you hear. Is it you or God?

4. Learn to submit to a community of believers. Only those who submit to others and can receive correction are healthy enough to prophesy (1Co 14:29).

5. Learn to recognize what God is doing in a service. Observe what's happening at the moment so you can weigh whether your word interrupts what God is saying or a work He is doing in those around you. When we say something can be as important as what we say.

6. Learn to ask whether that word is meant just for you. Ask yourself, "To whom is God speaking this word, and why?" Sometimes the word is for us, not everyone else.

7. Learn when to stop. Say what God gives you to say and then stop. Don't use a prophecy as an opportunity to preach to people (1Co 14:30).

8. Learn to be very careful about directive prophecies. In the New Covenant since God speaks to all, we don't need directive prophecies the way people

did in the centuries before Jesus. Avoid telling people what decisions to make in matters where the Bible is silent.

Conclusion

Moses longed for all of God's people to prophesy. Joel said a day would come when that would happen, and Peter stood up and said that because of Jesus that day had arrived. That means you and I can speak the word of the Lord. Yes, learning to prophesy can be intimidating, and we might make mistakes as we learn, but if we are willing to step out and try, maybe using some of the steps listed above, we will surely learn because the Holy Spirit dwells within us. And many people will be strengthened by this precious gift. May God's love for others constrain us to passionately desire to prophesy.

Chapter Nineteen

The Purpose of Tongues

*[7]Yet even lifeless things, either flute or harp, in producing a sound, if they
do not produce a distinction in the tones, how will it be known what is
played on the flute or on the harp? [8]For if the bugle produces an indistinct
sound, who will prepare himself for battle? [9]So also you, unless you utter by
the tongue speech that is clear, how will it be known what is spoken? For
you will be speaking into the air. [10]There are, perhaps, a great many kinds
of languages in the world, and no kind is without meaning. [11]If then I do
not know the meaning of the language, I will be to the one who speaks a
barbarian, and the one who speaks will be a barbarian to me. [12]So also
you, since you are zealous of spiritual gifts, seek to abound for the edification of the church. [13]Therefore let one who speaks in a tongue pray that he
may interpret. [14]For if I pray in a tongue, my spirit prays, but my mind
is unfruitful. [15]What is the outcome then? I will pray with the spirit and
I will pray with the mind also; I will sing with the spirit and I will sing
with the mind also. [16]Otherwise if you bless in the spirit only, how will
the one who fills the place of the ungifted say the "Amen" at your giving of
thanks, since he does not know what you are saying? [17]For you are giving
thanks well enough, but the other person is not edified. [18]I thank God, I
speak in tongues more than you all; [19]however, in the church I desire to
speak five words with my mind so that I may instruct others also, rather
than ten thousand words in a tongue.*

1 Corinthians 14:7-19

Those who seriously try to understand what Paul is saying in this section of his letter to the Corinthians can become quite confused. We can be misled by commentators, or even by the way certain verses are translated, until we find it very difficult to hear what Paul is actually saying. There has been so much resistance toward the subject of speaking in tongues in the academic world that those who look there for help may have been told that Paul didn't believe that tongues was really a language, that he actually wished that the Corinthians would stop speaking in tongues altogether, or that he thought it turns a person into a barbarian. Now, Paul did not say any of those things, but apparently it is what some people think he said. So it's no wonder that you and I may have struggled to learn what this passage really means. There has been a deliberate, longstanding campaign of distortion, and it's worked, and as a result the supernatural gifts of the Spirit have been almost completely absent in the majority of the church in the western world. Thankfully, the rapidly growing church in Asia, Africa and Latin America is largely pentecostal because these believers didn't listen to those commentaries but instead studied the Bible in a straightforward manner. And if the church in the western world is going to regain the vitality of the early church or of the non-western church, we need to remove this preconditioned thinking and let the Bible speak again. And the passage we're studying today is certainly no exception. We need to hear what Paul actually said to the Corinthians about speaking in tongues, and then you and I need to act on what our apostle teaches us because speaking in tongues isn't a useless gift. It isn't "the least of the gifts." It's a precious resource perfectly designed by God to accomplish exactly what He intended it to accomplish. And what is its purpose? Let's read this passage again because in it Paul answers that question in unmistakable terms.

What did Paul say?

Before we can understand the various statements Paul makes here, we need to remember why he wrote this passage. He wants the Corinthians to allow God's love to guide them in their use of the spiritual gifts (Greek: pneumatika, literal: spirituals, 14:1,12). And to illustrate this principle he selects two of those gifts, speaking in tongues and prophecy, and shows them how love should control their use. And as we will discover later in this chapter, he chose those two gifts because the Corinthians were especially misusing the gift of tongues in their gathered services. Apparently many of them were speaking in tongues loudly, all at once, and for significant amounts of time. The result was chaotic and frightened visitors, so in this passage Paul is teaching the church how to properly conduct a church service. He wants them to stop being selfish. They had been concerned only about edifying themselves, but he wants them to focus on edifying others. He has already told them his general opinion about tongues. He said, "I want you all to speak in tongues…" (v5), but in this passage he says that in church he wants them to restrain their speaking in tongues because that gift does not edify others unless it's translated into their own language. In that case, he says, speaking in tongues is just as edifying as prophecy.

So with this context in mind, let's listen as Paul continues to counsel the Corinthians. He has just asked them how helpful it would be if when he came to Corinth, he only spoke to them in tongues. And then he says this:

> "This principle of communication, that our words must be understood by someone else to be of help to them, can be illustrated by the use of musical instruments. Though the instruments themselves are lifeless objects, when someone plays an instrument properly, it too 'says' something that people can understand. Take for example a flute or a lute. If someone plays random notes that have no melody, how would a listener know what song is being played? Here's another example: In the military soldiers rely on a trumpeter to give them certain signals, but if someone picks up a trumpet and blasts disconnected sounds, no one will understand what that trumpet is saying, so no one will prepare for battle. Do you understand the point I'm making? If our words make no sense to those who are listening to us, we leave them in confusion. Unless the words we speak can be understood, we only make noise; we are speaking to no one; we are merely uttering sounds into the air. If we could count all the languages in the world, I'm sure we would find it is an enormous number, and not one of those languages is without meaning. But if I don't know the meaning of the words of that language, I become a foreigner to the person who is speaking it, and the person who is speaking becomes a foreigner to me.

"Because you are so zealous for the supernatural gifts of the Spirit, I want you to make a conscious effort to use those gifts to help everybody in the church, and if you will do that, the entire congregation will receive an abundance of ministry. Now, here's the guideline I want you to follow: If someone feels God is leading them to speak in a tongue in a service, because God wants everyone in that service to understand what will be said, before that person opens their mouth, I want him or her to ask God to give them the gift of interpreting tongues. That way he or she will understand the meaning of the words they are about to say and can then explain it to everyone afterward. Remember; when someone speaks in tongues, they normally don't know what they are saying. The Holy Spirit gives their human spirit words to pray to God, but their mind does not recognize the words. So here's what should happen: After a person has asked God to give them the translation or explanation (Ne 8:5-8) of what they are about to speak, that person may go ahead and pray out loud in the Spirit. Then when they are finished, they should interpret what was said. And this same procedure can also be done with singing in tongues to God. First, the person will sing the words the Holy Spirit gives them, and then they will sing the translation or explanation.

"If you don't obey this guideline, here's what will happen: Those who visit your services because they're curious or genuinely seeking to learn more about Jesus will have no idea what's going on when you are all speaking in tongues at once. All they will hear is a group of people talking in foreign languages, and even though each of you is blessing God and giving thanks to Him in the Spirit, they won't understand what you are saying or be able to participate. You will be praying well enough, but they won't be able to say, 'Amen' at the end of your prayer.

"By the way, in case you think I'm cautioning you in the use of speaking in tongues because I don't value this gift as much as you do, let me tell you how much I use this gift, personally. I give thanks to God that I speak in tongues more than all of you put together. My private devotional life is constantly filled

> with praying and singing in the Spirit, but when I'm in a church service, I would rather speak five words that teach others how to walk with God than stand in front of everyone and speak thousands of words in an unknown tongue. Why? Because God's love constrains me to do everything I possibly can to help others know Him better" (paraphrase).

The right words (vs 14-17)

If you and I look closely at what Paul says in this passage, particularly his statements in verses 14 through 17, we will discover that he indirectly reveals the content of what is being said when a person is speaking or singing in tongues. We learn here that they are either praying or praising, and Paul even describes how that happens. He says the Holy Spirit gives that person's spirit the right words to say to God at that moment, which raises the questions: Why would we need the Holy Spirit to help us pray or praise? And why would He cause us to say those things in a foreign language that our mind doesn't understand? I think the answer to these questions is found in Romans chapter eight and Exodus chapter two.

In the eighth chapter of Romans Paul compares believers in Jesus Christ to the people of Israel when they were still in bondage in Egypt. He does that by using the word <u>groan</u> (Ro 8:22-23, 26). He applies exactly the same word to the church that Moses used to describe Israel's misery in the second chapter of Exodus. Listen:

> "...And the sons of Israel sighed [Hebrew: groaned] because of the bondage, and they cried out; and their cry for help because of [their] bondage rose up to God. So God heard their groaning; and remembered His covenant with Abraham, Isaac, and Jacob" (Ex 2:23-24).

Groaning is a wordless sound that comes out of us when we are suffering. The Bible applies that word to people who are enduring childbirth, grieving for the dead, suffering physical pain, facing judgment or feeling sorrow for their sins. Even though it employs no words, the sound itself is full of meaning. It expresses the anguish of the heart; it communicates a longing for relief; it desperately cries out for someone to come and rescue us out of a terrible situation. And Moses says God heard the groaning of Israel and answered their cry for help.

So when Paul applies that same word, "groan" (Greek: stenazo) to us as believers, he is reminding us that, like Israel in Egypt, we're not in the promised land yet. We still live in the midst of a suffering creation and long to be free from the weaknesses and temptations that arise from our physical bodies, which is why we need the Holy Spirit to help us pray. Listen:

> "In the same way the Spirit also helps our weakness; for we do not know how to pray as we should, but the Spirit Himself intercedes [asks God to help us] for [us] with groanings too deep for words [unspoken groans]; and He who searches the hearts knows what the mind of the Spirit is, because He intercedes for the saints according to [the will of] God" (Ro 8:26-27).

These two verses provide a very important insight. Paul says believers tend to be weak because we don't know how to pray properly. Apparently, we often say the wrong things or don't say the right things at the right time. But here's the good news: Paul says the Holy Spirit has been given to us to help us pray. He literally prays for us. When we're groaning, He joins us. When we're confused, He prays the will of God. I realize this passage in Romans doesn't specifically mention speaking in tongues, but it does tell us that the Spirit has been sent to help us pray, and we've learned that speaking in tongues is Spirit-guided prayer and praise. So it seems impossible that these two passages don't have a connection. What Paul says the Spirit does in Romans must be part of what he says the Spirit does in First Corinthians. The One who groans on our behalf in Romans surely gives our spirit the right words to pray in the midst of our groaning in First Corinthians.

Conclusion

So far from being the "least of the gifts," speaking in tongues is probably the gift you and I need most often and most desperately. It's the words the Father is waiting to hear us say. It's the prayer and praise that will make us strong when we are weak. No wonder Paul prayed that way more than all of us. No wonder he was so strong when he went through such terrible trials (Ac 16:25). No wonder he wants us to have this gift too.

Chapter Twenty

When God is Silent

[20]Brethren, do not be children in your thinking; yet in evil be infants, but in your thinking be mature. [21]In the Law it is written, "By men of strange tongues and by the lips of strangers I will speak to this people, and even so they will not listen to Me," says the Lord. [22]So then tongues are for a sign, not to those who believe but to unbelievers; but prophecy is for a sign, not to unbelievers but to those who believe. [23]Therefore if the whole church assembles together and all speak in tongues, and ungifted men or unbelievers enter, will they not say that you are mad? [24]But if all prophesy, and an unbeliever or an ungifted man enters, he is convicted by all, he is called to account by all; [25]the secrets of his heart are disclosed; and so he will fall on his face and worship God, declaring that God is certainly among you.

1 Corinthians 14:20-25

The principle Paul teaches the Corinthians in this passage comes directly out of the Law of Moses. It's based on one of the curses God said Israel would endure if they disobeyed His covenant. Here's how the original warning was stated:

> "...because you would not obey the Lord your God by keeping His commandments and His statutes which He commanded you... The Lord will bring a nation against you from afar, from the end of the earth, as the eagle swoops down, a nation whose language you shall not understand..." (Dt 28:45-49).

Over the centuries the prophets, whose assignment was to remind Israel of the covenant they had made with God, would remind them of this particular curse. They warned that if the nation continued to violate the covenant, God would allow foreign armies to invade their land, and they would be ruled by soldiers whose language they did not understand. The basic point of that warning is this: If you stop listening to God's voice when He speaks to you in your own language through His prophets, at some point He will stop speaking and start disciplining. He will go silent and lift His protective hand. And the sign that this has happened will be the sound of a foreign language being spoken all around you by your new masters. Suddenly, in your own land, everywhere you turn you will hear the confusing babble of a language you don't understand. That noise will be God's way of saying, "I've stopped talking to you because you refused to listen to Me." Before Babylon invaded Judah, Jeremiah pointed to this particular curse and warned that this would happen. Listen:

> "'Behold, I am bringing a nation against you from afar, O house of Israel,' declares the Lord. 'It is an enduring nation, it is an ancient nation, a nation whose language you do not know, nor can you understand what they say'" (Jer 5:15).

Before Assyria invaded the northern kingdom of Israel, Isaiah pointed to the same curse and warned:

> "Indeed, He [God] will speak to this people through stammering lips and a foreign tongue, He who said to them, 'Here is rest, give rest to the weary,' and 'Here is repose,' but they would not listen" (Isa 28:11-12).

Both prophets were explaining an important truth about God: To those who listen and obey, He will speak to them in a language they understand, but to those who disobey and refuse to repent, at some point He will stop speaking, and that silence should serve as a warning that their heart has grown hard.

In my opinion, verses 20-25 are often improperly interpreted. People usually point to verse 22 to prove that speaking in tongues is a sign that will convince unbelievers that God is real. But then verse 23 seems to say the exact opposite, so it all ends up very confusing. I believe this confusion arises from the fact that the rabbinical nature of Paul's argument is overlooked. By quoting Isaiah 28:11 Paul is not quoting a verse out of context because it happens to mention speaking in "strange tongues." He was a very learned rabbi who understood the context in which Isaiah originally spoke those words. He knew Isaiah was warning Israel that God was about to cut off all meaningful communication because so many had refused to listen to Him. Their prophets would go silent, and they would be left to listen to the babble of foreign languages that were being spoken by the soldiers who had conquered them. He knew that in Isaiah's prophecy foreign tongues were a sign of judgment, not a reference to the fact that someday people would speak in tongues. So he quoted Isaiah's statement to correct a problem he identifies in verse twenty-three: "...if the whole church assembles together and all speak in tongues...." Apparently, when the Corinthians gathered for public services, they tended to speak in tongues all at once, probably in a loud voice, and probably for significant amounts of time. And it was that behavior Paul was trying to stop in these verses.

Unbelievers and believers (v22)

If we keep Isaiah's actual meaning in mind, Paul's comments in verse 22 make perfect sense and fit nicely into his argument against allowing uninterpreted tongues to dominate in a public service. The key is to understand what he means by the words "believers" and "unbelievers." The confusion stems from the fact that he uses the word "unbelievers" in two different ways. He uses it to mean one type of unbeliever in verse 22 and another type of unbeliever in verse 23. When he says in verse 22 that foreign tongues are a sign to <u>unbelievers</u>, he doesn't mean those who are not yet Christians; he means hard-hearted people who refuse to believe the things God has said to them. In other words, the same sort of unbeliever Isaiah was addressing. And when he says prophecy is not for unbelievers but <u>believers</u>, he means by the word "believer" those in the church with a tender heart who humbly listen to God when He speaks to them. Paul uses Isaiah's statement to explain to the Corinthians that when they all speak in foreign languages at once, and there is no interpretation, they produce a very wrong spiritual impression. From a biblical perspective, the babble of incomprehensible languages over God's people is a sign of judgment. It indicates that He has stopped communicating because they've stopped listening. But prophecy is reserved for those who are still willing to be corrected. And since the Corinthians weren't hard-hearted or under judgment when they held their public gatherings, the manner in which they were speaking in tongues needed to change. They needed to make room for God to speak to them. They needed to give preference to prophecy (14:1, 5).

Ungifted and unbelievers (v23)

In verse 23 Paul states the reason he wants the Corinthians to stop the practice of speaking in tongues in a loud voice, all at once, in their public services. He says the chaotic environment they were creating was causing visitors to think they had lost their minds. And here he uses the word "unbeliever" again, but this time he couples it with the word "ungifted" (NASB; Greek: idiotes, v16) which describes someone who has come into the service on their own initiative because they are curious or are seeking to know more about Jesus. So the unbeliever in this verse is a different category of "unbeliever" than the person in the preceding verse. The unbeliever in verse 22 is a stubborn person who knows what they are doing is wrong but refuses to be corrected, while the unbeliever in verse 23 is a visitor who doesn't believe because they haven't heard enough about Jesus to make a decision. This second type of unbeliever is not hardened or rebellious, just ignorant. When he or she comes into an assembly which is in proper order and hears a prophecy in their own language, their heart is able to open to the words they hear, and they are likely to respond by "falling on their face, worshiping God and declaring that God is among you" (vs24-25).

So to repeat what we have just said: To properly understand this passage, we must recognize the different ways Paul uses the word "unbeliever." The unbelievers in verse 22 are "unbelievers" because they have grown hard-hearted. They refuse to listen to God because they know what He's going to say and don't want to hear it. The unbelievers in verse 23 are "unbelievers" because they have not yet understood the gospel. In time God stops speaking to the first group, but He gladly speaks to the second group through His prophets to prove to them He is real.

When God is silent

The passage from Isaiah that Paul quotes to the Corinthian church contains a very serious truth. It warns that if a person refuses to listen to God long enough, He will stop speaking to them. At some point He will go silent. Though we may not recognize it during those painful moments when we are under conviction, the very fact that we can hear God rebuke us is a positive sign. It's a sign that our hearts are still soft. Listen to what Solomon told his son:

> "My son, do not reject the discipline of the Lord or loathe His reproof, for whom the Lord loves He reproves, even as a father [corrects] the son in whom he delights" (Pr 3:11-12).

When the Spirit grieves our heart, when a verse of Scripture shouts out a warning as we read it, when God sends someone to us with a word of correction, that communication, painful though it may be, means God considers us to be His child, and we've not lost our ability to hear Him. What we must learn to dread is not His discipline, for that is a sign of His love, but His silence because that is a sign that we have pushed our rebellion too far. He has decided that it's time to discipline us with hardship.

There is actually a progressive order to the way God disciplines His children. His first step is simply to speak to His child, preferably by the inner voice of the Holy Spirit through His written Word. And then, if we won't listen to those voices, He will send people to speak to us. These are His "prophets," and the person He uses might be a believer or an unbeliever, and the way we respond to these voices reveals whether we are wise or foolish in that particular area. Let's listen to Solomon again:

> "He who corrects a scoffer gets dishonor for himself, and he who reproves a wicked man [gets] insults for himself. Do not reprove a scoffer, or he will hate you, reprove a wise man and he will love you. Give [instruction] to a wise man and he will still be wiser, teach a righteous man and he will increase [his] learning. The fear of the Lord is the beginning of wisdom..." (Pr 9:7-10).

There are indeed individuals who don't fear God and have never submitted to Him, but Solomon's words don't apply only to them. I think they apply to those of us who serve Him yet still have areas in our lives where the Holy Spirit has confronted us but we stubbornly refuse to be corrected. When

He speaks to us about that particular matter, we don't listen, so in that area of our thinking we can be considered foolish. And the evidence that such an area exists is our refusal to listen to the voice of correction. Yet because God loves us and has ordained that we become like His Son (Ro 8:29), He will move to the next step: He will lift His protective hand and let us eat the bitter fruit of our disobedience. At first rebellion seems like liberation. We find joy in our sin. But when God tells us not to do a thing, it's because there is death of some kind in that action or attitude, and sooner or later we will reap what we've sown. Our sin will bring "death" in the form of broken relationships, lost jobs, ruined careers, destructive addictions, and probably most painful of all, a sense of shame when we come before God.

Now at this point I need to insert a note of caution because someone is likely to ask, "I'm going through hardship, does that mean I'm under discipline?" And here's how I would answer that question: All hardship is <u>not</u> discipline; in fact <u>most</u> hardship is not discipline. The person whom God is finally disciplining this way will know in their heart that He's the source of their hardship because they have deliberately refused His voice so many times. And if that's the case, the way out of that hardship is repentance. Once we release our stubborn rebellion and embrace His will, there is no need for further discipline. After we repent, God immediately begins to guide us out of that situation. Remember, His discipline isn't punishment; it's correction. It isn't meant to hurt us; it's meant to rescue us from something far worse (1Co 6:9-10).

There's a profound lesson here: As long as God is disciplining us, He is showing His love for us. The danger comes when He stops, when our conscience doesn't bother us anymore, when no one comes to confront us, when we feel "at peace" with a behavior the Bible clearly forbids. That's a sign that God's patience has run out, and we're headed for more severe discipline.

Conclusion

The disciplinary process we described today is for the first type of "unbeliever" that Paul mentions in this passage, not the second. It's how God deals with His rebellious children when they insist on doing things that could put their future with Him at risk. He doesn't deal this way with those who don't know Him. Yes, all sin brings hardship, but not all sin hardens the human heart. Some people are unaware of how God wants them to live, so their lifestyle, while definitely wrong in God's eyes, is not done defiantly. They are simply confused people trying to cope with life. That is very different than someone who knows what's right but chooses not to do it and then resists God's appeals to stop. The lesson that lies behind this passage is to repent quickly when God speaks to us and to recognize that His voice, even when confronting us, is a gift we must never take for granted. We never want His voice to become silent. We choose to listen carefully and repent quickly. Here's a beautiful truth that Paul told the Corinthians earlier in this letter:

> "But if we judged ourselves rightly, we would not be judged. But when we are judged, we are disciplined by the Lord so that we will not be condemned along with the world" (1Co 11:31-32).

Chapter Twenty-One

Freedom Within Order

26 What is the outcome then, brethren? When you assemble, each one has
a psalm, has a teaching, has a revelation, has a tongue, has an inter-
pretation. Let all things be done for edification. 27 If anyone speaks in a
tongue, it should be by two or at the most three, and each in turn, and one
must interpret; 28 but if there is no interpreter, he must keep silent in the
church; and let him speak to himself and to God. 29 Let two or three proph-
ets speak, and let the others pass judgment. 30 But if a revelation is made
to another who is seated, the first one must keep silent. 31 For you can all
prophesy one by one, so that all may learn and all may be exhorted; 32 and
the spirits of prophets are subject to prophets; 33 for God is not a God of con-
fusion but of peace, as in all the churches of the saints.... 40 But all things
must be done properly and in an orderly manner.

1 Corinthians 14:26-33, 40

Here is one of the foundational principles in the way God works with humans: He gives us freedom to choose and then asks us to exercise that freedom within specific boundaries. Time and again the troubles that enter our lives come because we use that freedom to do something that is outside His will. Our old human nature seems determined to test His boundaries. For some reason we question His motive for giving them to us. We may suspect that He forbids certain things because He's trying to deprive us rather than protect us. We assume that His rules are barriers that will prevent us from finding happiness, so we engage in behaviors and tolerate attitudes that He warned us would bring hardship, and as a result we suffer unnecessarily. In time we discover why He said what He did, but by then much damage may have already been done.

In light of all the suffering people bring upon themselves, someone might ask, "Why doesn't God simply force everyone to do the right thing, and then the world would be a much better place?" And that's true in one way; people would behave better. But that solution misses the point of why God created the human race. He made us "in His image" (Ge 1:27) so we could relate to Him as a Person, so we could become His children, not His slaves or His pets. For that relationship to exist He had to give us a measure of free will so we could choose to love Him and choose to obey Him. Without that freedom we would guide our lives by instinct, like animals, and that is not God's high purpose for us. In His great love He gave us the capacity to truly fellowship with Him. And freedom is an essential element for that capacity to exist. Without it we cannot love Him, and we cannot become like Him. But freedom also has a dark side. If we choose to use it badly, it can lead us to eternal ruin. Yet in God's thinking, the joy of fellowshipping forever with those who will come to Him is worth the sorrow of being separated from those who will not.

It doesn't take much reflection before you and I can identify dozens of areas where God has given us boundaries, or has shown us the proper way to handle a matter, and then asked us to obey Him. Through His written Word and the leading of the Spirit, He has provided us with instructions that touch on virtually every area of life, and that certainly includes what we do when we gather together to worship Him. In this passage we hear the apostle Paul asking believers in the city of Corinth to let the Holy Spirit guide them in the way they worship and to observe certain boundaries in the way they express His gifts. He tells them that if they will do what he asks, their services would inspire respect in visitors and model the peaceful character of God to all. As a result their gatherings would be powerful, beautiful and orderly. There would be enough freedom for each person to respond to the leading of the Holy Spirit, and there would be enough order to maintain a peaceful atmosphere. By writing these things, Paul presented the Corinthians with a choice: Would they submit to him, or would they continue to do what they had been doing? Let's try to understand what the apostle said to them, and then let's ask ourselves: Are we willing to exercise our freedom within the boundaries of God's order? Because if we are, we'll be able to continue to minister in that power and freedom for the rest of our lives.

Paul's instructions (1Co 14:26-33, 40)

Paul is writing to a church he had founded about five years earlier (Ac 18:1-18), and it's clear from what he writes in this letter that this church was not, at that time, being led by mature elders. In fact nowhere in his letters to Corinth does he even mention the existence of elders. It appears from his comments (1Co 1:10-13, 11:18) that the church had divided into quarreling factions with some claiming loyalty to Paul, some Apollos, some Peter (Cephas) and some Christ (meaning they followed no human leader). So Paul writes to try to heal these divisions and correct wrong behaviors, and in this portion of this letter (1Co 11-14) he is trying to correct mistakes they were making when they gathered for worship. After explaining some important principles about the nature of the church, beautifully describing the proper motivation for all ministry, and showing them an example of how love should guide them in the use of the spiritual gifts, Paul will now describe in general terms what a Spirit-led service should look like, in other words, how freedom can be expressed within order. Here's what I believe the Corinthians heard him say:

> "So now let's put all this together. Here's what will happen if you follow the principles I've taught you: The Holy Spirit will give each one of you a gift [or gifts] that will help others to carry the load they are bearing (1Co 12:7). For example, one of you might feel led to recite or sing a psalm. Someone else might feel led to share with everyone a truth that God has taught them. Another might receive a prophetic insight which becomes the starting point for a word of wisdom or knowledge or a prophecy. Someone else might feel led to speak in tongues in a voice loud enough for all to hear, and in that case that person or someone else would need to interpret that tongue so everyone could understand the prayer or praise that was just spoken. Remember: In a service the gifts of the Spirit should be used to help others.

"If there are going to be tongues in a service, I don't want more than two or, at the most, three in a row before you stop and allow someone to interpret each one. And each person should be given sufficient time to share their gift. If there is no one present in the meeting who is capable of interpreting a tongue, let those who have that gift remain silent. They may speak in tongues quietly to themselves, at a volume others can't hear, but of course God always hears what your spirit is saying. As I told you earlier (v13), each person who wishes to speak out in a tongue should ask God to give them the interpretation before they start, but if that person is unable to interpret their tongue, it is permissible for someone else to interpret it for them.

"If two or three prophets speak, one after the other, before any other gifts are expressed, stop and ask those who are spiritually mature to evaluate what was said. Was there anything in those prophecies that violated Scripture? Was a prophecy presented with a wrong attitude? Was God actually directing those words to the whole church or to just an individual? If someone is prophesying and speaks so long that someone else receives a word while they are still talking, the first person should sit down and let the next person speak. I would prefer not to have prophecies go on too long. It is better if they are brief and to the point. And it is unacceptable to have two people prophesying at the same time. No one should start prophesying while someone else is still speaking. If you follow these guidelines, everyone will have a chance to share what the Spirit is leading them to say, and as a result the church will be taught and receive encouragement.

"Someone might say to me, 'Paul, I want to follow your guidelines, but when the Spirit comes over me, He compels me to speak, and I can't help myself.' But that's not true. The Holy Spirit doesn't overwhelm a person so that they have no control over what they are saying. Yes, the Spirit supplies the words that you speak, but you are able to start and stop when you want to. It's not like the prophets you used to listen to in pagan temples.

The Holy Spirit doesn't compulsively force a person to blurt something out.

"These boundaries I'm giving you will not quench the work of God because the God of the Bible, the One who has sent the Holy Spirit to you through Jesus Christ, is not a God of disorder [anarchy, confusion], but of peace [joyful harmony]. So my goal in all of this is to have your services properly reflect His character. And you need to know that no other church in the world functions in the chaotic way in which you have been functioning. I travel continually and stay in touch with congregations everywhere, and yours is the only one whose services are full of disunity and confusion. It's very important that you listen to me. Don't listen to those who try to overrule me by claiming to be prophets or saying they are acting on a word from the Lord. I want you to follow my guidelines, and if you do, your services will have a beauty that causes the community to respect the way you worship, and there will be an orderly flow of the gifts of the Spirit with one ministry following another (paraphrase)."

Paul's principles

Though Paul was correcting the Corinthian church and even said, in effect, there was no other church in the world that behaved the way they did, his concern was <u>not</u> that they were zealous for the things of the Spirit, in particular speaking in tongues. His concern was that they were expressing those gifts without love, in a way that ignored the needs of the visitors who came into their services to learn about Jesus, and they were creating a spiritual environment that did not reflect the peaceful character of God. His goal was not to persuade them to stop expressing the gifts of the Spirit but to do so in a beautiful and orderly way. And in the course of this discussion he taught them a number of foundational principles that apply to the Lord's Church in every generation, not only first-century Corinth. And since he is our apostle as much as he was theirs, let's reflect on these foundational principles so we can obey him, and he would be pleased if he walked into our worship services today. He said:

1. The Holy Spirit is the rightful leader of every service.

2. He will give certain gifts to certain people, and there is no way of knowing who that will be until the service is underway. He will distribute His gifts "to each one… just as He wills" (1Co 12:11).

3. Every believer should come to church expecting the Spirit to give them a gift to share with someone else (1Co 12:7, 11, 18; 14:26).

4. The Holy Spirit knows the needs of the congregation and will distribute a variety of gifts to meet those needs.

5. Believers must be aware of visitors who don't know Jesus yet. Our highest goal must be evangelism, not personal edification. We can edify our own spirit at other times.

6. Every gift is to be tested. No one is above evaluation. When we present a gift, we submit it to the congregation for their approval or rejection.

7. People who are yielded to the Holy Spirit do not lose their self-control. The "… spirits of prophets are subject to prophets" (1Co 14:32).

8. Guidelines for the gifts of the Spirit are needed to protect the church from being dominated by our human flesh.

9. Beauty and order: The Holy Spirit is not leading if a service is disorderly, and people are becoming confused. When He leads, the Holy Spirit will present His gifts in a way that is beautiful, and even visitors who don't understand the gifts will respect what's happening. When He's leading, everyone can receive a blessing.

Paul's goals

Some people say that if you try to pastor the gifts of the Spirit you will quench them, and that is certainly possible. If someone doesn't have Paul's heart, one which truly loved the gifts of the Spirit, then even the foundational principles we've just seen can be used in a harsh way to smother the gifts. But the reason Paul taught these things was not to prevent the Corinthians from moving freely in the Spirit, but to protect them from making certain mistakes that in time would cause the church and community to despise the gifts. Without guidelines human flesh always takes over and ruins something God intended to be beautiful. In fact, it appears that very thing had happened to the church in Thessalonica. Listen to what Paul felt the need to say to them:

> "Do not quench the Spirit; do not despise prophetic utterances. But examine everything [carefully]; hold fast to that which is good…" (1Th 5:19-21).

Paul was pastoring the gifts in Corinth not to <u>prevent</u> them but to <u>preserve</u> them. If done wrongly, they would soon cease; if done properly, they would continue to be a blessing to everyone. And that is still true today.

Section Three

The Order of Future Events

This brief, but important, section reminds us that the baptism with the Holy Spirit is an essential part of God's great plan of salvation. In this final chapter we review the biblical order of future events, and as we do, it becomes evident that our relationship with the Holy Spirit is destined to only grow deeper and stronger with the passing of time. By giving us this "baptism," Jesus not only equips us to be His witnesses in this present age, but He moves us a step closer to the glorious future that God has prepared for us. He restores the original relationship with the Spirit that we lost in the garden of Eden and gives us a foretaste of the glory we will someday experience at levels beyond anything we can now imagine.

And there will no longer be any night;
and they will not have need of the light of a lamp
nor the light of the sun,
because the Lord will illumine them...

Revelation 22:5

Chapter Twenty-Two

God's Prophetic Plan

This isn't it. We haven't arrived. In fact, we've only just begun. The future God has planned for us will be filled with more and more of the Holy Spirit until His presence reaches a level of intensity that if we were to experience it today, before receiving our resurrection bodies, it would consume us. What God has given us in this season of history is wonderful, but compared to what we will have in the ages to come, it is described by Paul as only a "first fruits" of a much larger harvest (Ro 8:23) and by the author of Hebrews as a "foretaste of the powers of the age to come" (Heb 6:5). We are grateful for what God has given us now, and we want to learn to walk in the Spirit now as deeply as we can. But we are still waiting for more.

When we study our Bible, the whole Bible, both the Old and the New Testaments, we soon discover that it reveals a very specific plan concerning the future of the world and our future. In surprising detail God explains how He will bring this present age to an end, and what will take place after that. It seems the only information He chooses to withhold are specific names and dates. Through His prophets, apostles and especially our Lord Jesus, He opens to us the deep counsels of His heart concerning the future, and I believe He does this for a very important reason: not to satisfy our curiosity, but to steady us. He wants us to recognize where we are in His great plan and to be confident of where we're headed. He wants us to see our lives from His perspective because His perspective is what will help us endure through hardship. When things seem to be going in the wrong direction, when it seems that God isn't being glorified, when darkness seems to be conquering light, He lifts us up and shows us the situation as He sees it: merely a passing moment on His prophetic timetable. And that perspective fills us with hope, and it's hope that fills us with joy, and it's the joy of the Lord that restores our strength.

In this final chapter we will look at the main elements of the prophetic plan God has laid out in the Bible. We'll begin with the rejection of Jesus and move forward through time until we arrive at the new heaven and the new earth. And remember, we're not doing this to satisfy our curiosity, but to steady us. You and I need this perspective as much as the early church did, maybe more. We too need to remember that God is completely in control of the course of human history. No, He's not responsible for the evil choices people make, but in spite of those choices, He is able to guide all things toward His great goal which is to draw from the human race a family of sons and daughters who will become exactly like Jesus in character and glory. And He won't allow the flow of history to end until every last soul who will come has come.

The order of future events

In order to understand the meaning of a particular prophecy about the future that we might encounter as we read through the Bible, we need to know where it fits in God's prophetic plan. There is a proper order to those events, and unless we recognize where that passage belongs in God timetable, what we're reading will be confusing. One passage talks about future blessings while another talks about judgment. One passage warns of a coming war while another pictures peace. One passage describes the sufferings of a dying Messiah while another proclaims that a glorious Messiah is coming to rule in power. And without understanding the master plan behind it all, we won't know how these very different events fit together.

I realize that there are many opinions about what the proper order of these events should be, but the following sequence is the order that I believe the Bible presents. And I'll start with an overlooked statement by Jesus concerning His rejection:

The rejection of Jesus: Matthew and Luke record a statement Jesus made shortly before His betrayal and arrest. Speaking to a crowd in Jerusalem He said:

> "Jerusalem, Jerusalem, who kills the prophets and stones those who are sent to her! How often I wanted to gather your children together, the way a hen gathers her chicks under her wings, and you were unwilling. Behold, your house is being left to you desolate! For I say to you, from now on you will not see Me until you say, 'Blessed is He who comes in the name of the Lord!'" (Mt 23:37-39; also Lk 13:34-35).

Israel's religious leaders, and those who followed them, rejected Jesus' message that the Messiah must suffer and die. Apparently they would have welcomed Him if He had used His power to overthrow the occupying Roman army, but He refused to do that. Instead He insisted that He must die as a sacrifice for their sins, so even as He spoke the words quoted above, they had already formed a plan to kill Him.

Though this statement is often overlooked as a part of God's prophetic timetable, I think it reveals that had Israel's leaders responded differently, the promised restoration described in many Old Testament passages would have begun, and God would have evangelized the Gentile world differently than the way we read about in the book of Acts. Certain things, such as the cross, had to happen, but apparently events would have unfolded differently if the nation's leaders had "...recognized the time of (their) visitation" (Lk 19:44). And the result of that rejection was that the spiritual restoration of Israel was postponed (Isa 52:7-10).

The crucifixion, resurrection and ascension: Jesus fulfilled His role as the sacrifice for our sins; God vindicated Him by raising Him from the dead and then physically lifted Him up into heaven and placed all things under His authority. From there Jesus sent the Holy Spirit to indwell His followers.

The first Pentecost: Peter introduced the arrival of the baptism with the Holy Spirit as the beginning of the promised restoration of Israel (Ac 2:16-21) which the prophet Joel, among others, had said would take place before a time of great tribulation for the nation (Joel 2:28-3:2). Yet many in Israel rejected their Messiah when He came and refused to believe the gospel when it was proclaimed to them. So the "favorable year of the Lord" (Lk 4:17-21; Isa 61:1-2) that belonged to Israel, first of all, became instead a prolonged harvest of Gentiles. And that harvest has continued for nearly two thousand years.

The restoration of Israel: But God never stops pursuing His plan of salvation; He simply reaches His goal another way. And from Moses onward (Dt 30:1-9), the prophets declared that there would be a season of regathering Jews into their homeland, of restoring the strength and prosperity of the nation of Israel, of corporate repentance toward God and of a great outpouring of God's Spirit upon all of God's people, both men and women, young and old (Isa 54, 55, 60-66; Jer 31; Eze 36, 37; Joel 2, 3; Ro 11). And though, as we've just seen above, this outpouring on Israel was interrupted the first time, it will not be interrupted again. Along with the physical restoration of Israel, there will be another, even greater spiritual restoration (an even greater Pentecost). And in this restoration Jesus will no longer be seen by Israel as a false teacher, but as the promised Savior that He is. Works righteousness will give way to the righteousness that comes by faith in Him. People will place their trust in Jesus' sacrifice on the cross. And this widespread spiritual renewal, along with jealousy because of the nation's growing prosperity, will provoke a coalition of Gentile nations to attack Israel, and that assault will culminate in a war that is prophesied over and over again in the Scriptures (Isa 29:1-8; 34:1ff; Eze 38:17-23; Zec 12:2-9; 14:2-9). The antichrist's army will invade Israel, surround Jerusalem and capture it (Zec 14:2), but then God will begin to fight to defend His people.

The return of the Messiah: When it looks like all is lost, a series of remarkable events will occur. To begin with, a resurrection will take place during which all the righteous dead will be clothed with their immortal bodies. Those believers who are alive and living on the planet at the time will also be clothed with their resurrection bodies and then be caught up into the air to join the great host of angels and resurrected humans who are accompanying Jesus as He returns to the earth. His arrival will initiate the destruction of the forces that had invaded Israel (Da 12:1; Zec 12:8; 14:4; Mt 24:29-31; 1Th 4:15-17; Rev 19:11-12). Joel 3:2 calls this event "the valley of Jehoshaphat" ("Yahweh judges"); the apostle John calls it "Armageddon" (Rev 16:16) and "the great winepress of the wrath of God" (Rev 14:19-20).

The Messianic kingdom: After these enemy forces are destroyed, Jesus will set up His throne in Jerusalem and rule over the entire earth for one thousand years (Rev 20:6-7). Those who were resurrected will rule with Him extending His authority and ministry as His representatives. The planet will still be populated with mortal humans who will continue to bear children and die (Isa 65:20, 22), and who will still have the opportunity to receive Jesus as their Savior. Jesus Himself will be physically present on earth, and His throne will be in Jerusalem. During this "millennium" the mortal human population will be forced to live righteously (Isa 2:1-4; Zec 14:16-19). Jesus' government and ministry will be extended to the entire planet through His resurrected followers who will "...reign with Him for a thousand years" (Rev 20:6). And the earth will be immersed in a very intense level of the presence of the Holy Spirit (Isa 11:9; Hab 2:14), one which is so strong that the curse which has been upon the earth and the animal world will be removed (Isa 11:6-8; 55:13; 65:25).

The final war: At the end of this thousand-year period, God will test the mortal human population by releasing the devil from the abyss into which he had been placed (Rev 20:1-3). Even though the reality and goodness of Jesus will be unquestionable during that season, the Tempter will again be allowed to stir rebellion against Him. And this will produce a resuscitation of the antichrist's kingdom, and its armies will again surround Jerusalem and prepare to attack. But this time the attack won't be allowed. Before it happens, fire will come down from heaven and destroy the invading armies (Rev 20:7-9).

The second resurrection and the judgment: Then God will begin His final judgment. The devil, the antichrist and the false prophet will be dealt with first. Then the unrighteous dead will be resurrected and judged according to a written record of their lives (Da 12:2; Jn 5:28-29; Rev 20:11-13). And finally, death itself, as well as the very place where the spirits of the unrighteous dead had been waiting for this moment of judgment, will be sent into the fire of God.

The release of God's glory: Up until the moment when the final judgment takes place, God will restrain the glorious fire of His holiness. That brilliant light that blinded Paul (Ac 9:3-8) and left Moses' face shining (Ex 34:29-35) contains an energy that must be restrained or it will destroy the created universe. Only in heaven can it shine freely. But at the final judgment a threshold will be passed that allows His glory to finally be released. And John was shown that moment in a vision. After seeing the Lord take His throne, John said, "…earth and heaven fled away, and no place was found for them" (Rev 20:11). That means that they will disappear and never return. John seems to be telling us that when the unrestrained glory of God is released, it will literally evaporate the created universe to make way for a new one.

The new heaven and earth: And finally, the apostle John was also shown "a new heaven and a new earth" (Rev 21:1). God will create a new universe that is able to withstand the impact of His unrestrained presence. In effect, the creation itself must also be "resurrected," remade of materials which are immortal so that, like our resurrected bodies, it can endure in a future so full of the Holy Spirit that there will be no need for a sun or moon to give light (Rev 21:23).

Conclusion

When we listen to Jesus or the apostles or the great prophets of Israel, we hear people who have a very clear picture in their minds of what will happen next in God's prophetic plan for human history. Their understanding of "tomorrow" was so distinct, so tangible, so beautiful that it dramatically changed the way they lived "today." But somewhere over the course of the centuries those understandings of God's prophetic plan have been lost. Many of us open up our Bibles and are confused by what we read. We see prophetic passages but don't know where they fit in God's timeline, so we don't know what they mean, and as a result we tend to ignore what the Bible says about our future. Yet if you and I are going to live our lives well and face death boldly, we need to understand God's plan. No, we don't need to know all the details. We don't need to spend our time guessing names and dates, but we do need to understand the larger plan that God has chosen to reveal because that knowledge has a powerful impact. It gives us perspective. It reminds us that this age in which we are now living is passing away. It reminds us that the future God has planned for us will be filled with more and more of the Holy Spirit. It reminds us that the baptism with the Holy Spirit, as wonderful as it is, is only a "foretaste of the powers of the age to come." And that perspective fills us with hope, and hope fills us with joy, and it's the joy of the Lord that restores our strength.

Small Group Discussion Questions

The following questions do not provide a thorough study guide. They've been included only as a possible help for small-groups that choose to discuss this book chapter by chapter or as an aid to the individual reader who wishes to personally interact with the main topics found in each chapter.

Chapter 1: The Holy Spirit

1) If you were teaching a Sunday School class for children and your assignment was to explain the Holy Spirit, what would you say?

2) In those challenging moments when you need the Holy Spirit to guide or strengthen you, what do you do? Give an example of a situation in which He helped you.

Chapter 2: The Promise of the Spirit

1) Have you asked the Holy Spirit to come to dwell within you? If so, did He come? How do you know? What changes in yourself have you observed?

2) What would you say to a believer who says, "I have sinned, and I think God has left me"? What scriptures would you point to? What would you tell that person to do?

Chapter 3: Introducing Jesus (Jn 1:19-37)

1) Pick one of the four essential truths that John the Baptist proclaimed about Jesus and explain why that truth is important to you.

2) Which of these four truths has been the most difficult for you to understand? Have you heard conflicting opinions about it? Have you found an answer?

Chapter 4: The Spirit Arrives (Ac 2:1-21, 37-39)

1) Read Acts 2:33. Where is Jesus now? Why do we call Him the "Baptizer with the Holy Spirit?"

2) Read Acts 2:41-42. How did those who believed Peter's message respond that day? What four activities became a regular part of their daily lives? How can we practice those same activities today?

Chapter 5: Receiving the Spirit

1) Have you received the Baptism with the Holy Spirit? If so, please describe when and how.

2) Did someone help you receive the Baptism with the Holy Spirit, or were you alone? Were there obstacles or issues you had to deal with first? If so, how were those removed?

Chapter 6: Giving God Our Tongue (Ac 2:1-21)

1) If you are able to speak in tongues, would you mind telling us about the first time you did that? What did you experience that day?

2) How often do you speak in tongues? How does it help you?

Chapter 7: Helping Others Receive the Gift of Tongues

1) What are some reasons that can cause people to be afraid to speak in tongues?

2) Have you ever helped someone else receive the Baptism with the Holy Spirit and step out in the gift of tongues? If so, please describe that moment. What did you say; what did you do, and how did that person respond?

Chapter 8: The Perfect and the Partial (1Co 13:8-13)

1) Read John 14:12. Was Jesus giving this promise only to His twelve disciples or to all believers? What kind of "works" did Jesus do?

2) Have you ever given a prophecy or spoken in tongues or had a word of knowledge in a gathering of believers? If so, tell us about it. Who was helped by it?

Chapter 9: The New You (Eze 36:25-27)

1) Which of these three truths has God been speaking to you lately? Why is that truth important to you?

2) Can you think of a time when the Holy Spirit strengthened you and helped you walk through a difficult trial?

3) What steps did you take that helped you receive His strength? How did He help you?

Chapter 10: Walking in the Spirit

1) What are some of the common warning signs that indicate that you have slipped into the "flesh?"

2) Do you have any daily disciplines that help you draw close to God (worship, prayer, Bible reading/listening)?

3) If you knew that you had to minister to someone an hour from now, what would you do to spiritually prepare yourself?

4) What does the presence of the Holy Spirit feel like to you?

Chapter 11: His Seal and Pledge (Eph 1:13-14)

1) If you have personally received the Baptism with the Holy Spirit, how did that experience change the way you think about God? How did it change the way you think about yourself?

2) Think of a time when you felt very close to God. When was it? What led you into that encounter? What did His presence feel like? Can you imagine what it will be like to be in His presence forever?

Chapter 12: Testing Prophecy (1Co 12:1-3)

1) Have you ever heard a false prophecy? At what point did you realize it was false? How did that experience affect you?

2) Have you ever given a prophetic word (word of knowledge, word of wisdom, prophecy, a specific Scripture verse or a biblical event)? Did it come in words, pictures, feelings or a verse of Scripture? How did you know when to stop?

Chapter 13: When We Gather (1Co 12:4-11)

1) Think of a time when you were worshiping in a church service, and God spoke to you or ministered to you in a special way. If you're comfortable doing so, please tell us what you heard, or what you felt.

2) Think of a time when God used you to minister to another believer? What did you do? What did you say?

3) Look over Paul's list of "the gifts of the Spirit" in verses eight through ten. Pick one that you have experienced and describe what God did.

Chapter 14: The Body of Christ (1Co 12:12-27)

1) If someone asked you why there are so many different kinds of people in your church, what would you say?

2) Have you identified your call to ministry? Has God given you compassion for a specific area of human need? What is it? In what ways have you reached out to help those who have that need?

Chapter 15: Guided by Love (1Co 12:27-13:3)

1) What is the kindest, most loving thing you've ever seen another person do? How did that act of kindness affect you?

2) Pick out a story in the Bible that describes someone who did something that models agape love. What selfless decision did that person make? Why do you think they made it?

3) Think of an example where Paul modeled this kind of love. Name something he did or said that reminds you of Jesus.

Chapter 16: The Spirit's Assignment (1Co 13:4-7)

1) Have you ever seen "heroic love" in action? Have you been present when someone put their life on the line to save someone else? Have you ever put yourself in danger to save someone else?

2) Look through the list of things that love does and pick one that you have done yourself. Tell us what you did and why.

3) Did you notice a change in your attitude toward others when you met Jesus? Describe that change if you can.

Chapter 17: Love Never Falls (1Co 13:8-13)

1) If someone asked you, "What will happen to me after I die?" what would you say?

2) What's the difference between "heaven" and the "age to come?"

3) Think of a time when you, in effect, asked yourself the question, "What would love do?" What was the decision that you faced? What choice did you make?

Chapter 18: Learning to Prophesy (1Co14:1-6)

1) Have you received a prophetic word from someone else that turned out to be absolutely true? If it's not too personal, would you share that word with us?

2) Have you ever received a prophetic word from someone else that turned out to be wrong? Without mentioning anyone's name, how did that experience affect you? What did you learn?

3) Has God asked you to give a prophetic word to another person? Can you share that word with us? How did the person respond?

Chapter 19: The Purpose of Tongues (1Co 14:7-19)

1) Can you think of a time when the situation you were facing was so challenging that you didn't know how to pray? What did you do?

2) If someone asked you, "What is the purpose of speaking in tongues?" what would you say?

3) Based on what Paul taught us, what would you expect to hear when a "tongue" is interpreted (translated into your own language)? Have you ever heard someone do this?

Chapter 20: When God is Silent (1Co 14:20-25)

1) In these verses what were the Corinthians doing in their church services that Paul is asking them to stop? What are the two reasons he gives for what that behavior is wrong?

2) Was Paul against speaking in tongues? Did he do it himself? How did he want speaking in tongues to be handled in a public service?

3) Think of a time when God told you to stop doing something. How did you hear His voice? Did you obey right away? If not, what finally convinced you to obey?

4) Have you ever needed to go through hardship before you were able to repent? If it's not too personal would you share with us what you learned from that experience?

Other Books by
Dr. Steve Schell

Study Verse by Verse: Romans
Study Verse by Verse: Acts
Preaching Through Romans

Contact Information

Life Lessons Publishing is a Registered Trade
Name for Pastoral Resource Ministry

lifelessonspublishing.com

info@lifelessonspublishing.com

Chapter 21: Freedom Within Order (1Co 14:26-33, 40)

1) When you go to church, do you expect the Holy Spirit to give you a gift to share with someone else? If so, how do you spiritually prepare yourself so you will be able to hear Him when He speaks to you?

2) Have you been in a service that was both free in the Spirit and orderly? Please describe what happened and how you felt during that service.

Chapter 22: God's Prophetic Plan

1) Look up Joel 2:28-32, then using the outline provided in this lesson, explain the events that Joel is describing.

2) Do you see events taking place in the world today which seem to fit in God's prophetic plan? Name one and show where it fits in the outline.

3) What event on this list brings the most hope and joy to your heart?